THE NOTORIOUS ESG

THE NOTORIOUS ESG

Business, Climate, and the Race to Save the Planet

BY

VASUKI SHASTRY

United Kingdom – North America – Japan
India – Malaysia – China

Emerald Publishing Limited
Howard House, Wagon Lane, Bingley BD16 1WA, UK

First edition 2023

Reprints and permissions service
Contact: permissions@emeraldinsight.com

British Library Cataloguing in Publication Data
A catalogue record for this book is available from the British Library

ISBN: 978-1-80455-545-3 (Print)
ISBN: 978-1-80455-542-2 (Online)
ISBN: 978-1-80455-544-6 (Epub)

INVESTOR IN PEOPLE

For my late mother, and to Singapore.

TABLE OF CONTENTS

Also by the Author   ix

About the Book   xi

1. The ABC of ESG   1

2. A Brief History of Grime   17

3. Our Carbon-Industrial Complex   31

4. The Prophet Motive   49

5. Emission Omissions   65

6. The Merits of "Woke" Capitalism   81

7. Bored of Directors   103

8. Rebels Without a Pause   119

9. Making ESG Great Again   135

Epilogue – The Interviews   153

Acknowledgments   163

Index   165

About the Author   171

ALSO BY THE AUTHOR

Has Asia Lost It? Dynamic Past, Turbulent Future (2021)
Resurgent Indonesia – From Crisis to Confidence (2018)

ABOUT THE BOOK

In terms of sheer hype, hoopla, and hysteria, ESG (or environmental, social, governance) has become the operating mantra for business in the developed and developing world. CEOs and C-suites have embraced ESG as the defining new way of doing business, underpinned by strong social purpose and a clear objective of doing well by doing good. The urgent, immediate global challenge of tackling climate change has raised the stakes with greater pressure to dismantle our carbon-industrial complex. The business community in America and Europe is also buffeted by unprecedented social pressures with demands from a millennial workforce for greater equity, diversity, and flexible working arrangements. Derided in some quarters as "woke capitalism," the adaptive challenge for business is to not merely to manage ESG risks but to fundamentally transform business models. In his new book, ESG expert Vasuki Shastry argues that short termism still rules, and unless the modern corporation radically changes to address environmental and social challenges, ESG will continue to remain notorious, infused with high prose and rhetoric, and with little substance and credibility. Citing Einstein, Shastry defines the current business approach toward ESG as driven by fear, greed, and stupidity. Fear, because businesses are feeling greater pressure to reform from investors and regulators. Greed, because ESG is also proving to be a massive business opportunity as the rise of sustainable finance attests. Stupidity, because every well-meaning corporate endeavor, however virtuous, will inevitably lead to excess. Making ESG great again will require bold ambition, a resolute commitment to curb greenwashing, and to include the voices and perspectives' of millennial staff, who stand to inherit a planet in grave climate peril. The generation gap is exemplified by the typical CEO of a modern corporation who is male, in his 50s, ruthlessly focused on delivering for the quarter, and hopelessly out of touch with environmental and social issues. A starting point for reform is greater diversity at the top and an acknowledgment that ESG should be the ABC of doing business.

1

THE ABC OF ESG

What Is Driving the Hype, Hoopla, and Hysteria of Environmental, Social, Governance (ESG).

In the 1970s at the height of disco mania, *Time* magazine memorably described the phenomenon as the "noun, verb, and adjective" of the decade. As corporate gurus look back on the present decade, there are likely to be many contenders for the noun, verb, and adjective label of our times. The pandemic certainly looms large and so would the current crypto mania. However, in terms of sheer hype, hoopla, and hysteria in the business world, the rise of environmental, social, governance (ESG) would be the top contender for the label.

In an era of social media memes, Twitter trolls, and fake news, ESG has proven to be bullet proof by rallying the most cynical corporate tycoon, millennial staff, and the NGO sector around the proposition that business can do well by doing good. "Business can in fact be a tremendous force for good and make a huge contribution to solving the biggest problems facing our people and planet," says Paul Polman, former CEO of Unilever.[1] "Actually, this is the only way for business to be accepted in society, and it should always strive to have a net positive impact." During his tenure as Unilever chief, Polman positioned sustainability as the

---

[1]Polman made these remarks to Mongabay, the environmental science and conservation news platform, October 19, 2020.

centerpiece of the consumer food giants strategy and also playing a critical role in rallying business around the United Nation's Sustainable Development Goals (SDGs) in 2015.[2]

Since the launch of the SDGs, business interest in all things development, climate, and ESG have soared. But as this book will argue, sustaining this interest over a longer period is already proving to be challenging. For now, the primacy of shareholder and shareholder value, the iron-clad governing principle of business in America and Europe for decades has been replaced by stakeholder capitalism, something fuzzier and harder to define because it promises to be all things to all people. Shareholder and stakeholder interests do align in the long term, according to Bruce Simpson, a senior ESG[3] advisor of McKinsey, "If you have happy employees, collaborative suppliers, satisfied regulators, and devoted consumers, then they will help you deliver higher benefits over a longer-term period." However, he acknowledges that it is hard to satisfy everybody in the short-term: you have to make trade-offs between purpose and profit. "But in the long term, we don't believe this trade-off exists."

For now, the burgeoning ESG Consultants Complex is bursting over with keywords and phrases – social purpose, responsible business, sustainability, greenwashing – which I hope to unpack in the next few chapters. Integrated reporting, an entirely new way of presenting financial and nonfinancial performance has become all the rage. Sustainability standard-setters, in the private and public sectors, are falling over each other in presenting templates to better measure impact. No ESG conversation is complete in New York, London, or Berlin without someone speaking about the merits of the Sustainability Accounting Standard Board's materiality matrix or the Task-Force for Climate-Related Disclosures (TCFD), which is aimed at getting sharper and precise climate data from listed companies, or the European Union's incredibly complex taxonomy

[2]For the uninitiated, the UN membership adapted 17 Sustainable Development Goals in 2015, a "shared blueprint for peace and prosperity."
[3]Putting stakeholder capitalism into practice – McKinsey podcast, January 7, 2022.

for sustainable activities. For business itself, their approach toward ESG is being defined by what Einstein[4] once described as three of the "great forces" ruling the world – fear, greed, and stupidity. Fear, because businesses are feeling the pressure from investors and regulators and don't want to be left behind in the ESG race; Greed, because ESG is also a massive business opportunity as the rise of sustainable finance demonstrates, with an estimated $3 trillion of assets under management and attendant concerns over green-washing, which we will discuss later; Stupidity, because every corporate endeavor, however virtuous it might seem, will inevitably lead to excess.

There are the skeptics and the cynics of course, who dismiss the entire phenomenon as "woke capitalism" or worse a "scam," as Elon Musk memorably described it after his electric car company Tesla was excluded from the S&P ESG Index, with oil major Exxon Mobil still in it. In short, business appears to have a love-hate relationship with ESG with plenty of lovers and plenty of haters. As a polarizing topic, ESG just about mirrors the world we live in.

Before we delve in-depth into this topic, it is useful to describe what exactly I mean by the business community, which I will reference throughout the book. It is an expansive term to describe the traditional private sector in Europe and America – the conglomeration of listed and unlisted companies involved in every imaginable (and unimaginable) business activity. This includes heavyweights in the Fortune 500 and leading businesses in Europe which span the globe and comprise the modern tribe of the multi-national corporation. It includes the financiers, the technologists, the service providers, the manufacturers, energy generators, and new generation upstarts who seek to disrupt all of the above.

The definition of what comprises the business community gets cloudy and murkier the further afield one travels from the shores of America and Europe. China has shown the way in recent years that state-owned capitalism can be a worthy counterweight and competitor to traditional Western free enterprise-driven capitalism. While China does have a genuine group of purely private

---

[4]The quote by Einstein is widely cited, including in *The Guardian*, October 23, 2008 (Fear is the new mindset of the irrational world of finance).

enterprises, the tech majors Alibaba, Tencent stand out in this regard, recent efforts by Beijing to curtail their power signals that state capitalism will dominate in the years ahead. State-owned enterprises in China, India, Indonesia, Mexico, Brazil, Nigeria, and other emerging markets coexist side by side with the private sector but dominate economic activity and are large consumers of capital and labor. They are typically involved in energy and finance, giving the politicians and technocrats who run these enterprises, vast power and privileges. While purists will fulminate at my rather expansive definition of what constitutes a modern business enterprise, it would be a mistake to exclude state-owned firms from the mix of firms who can provide solutions to mitigating climate change and in overall ESG compliance. In my book both purely private and purely state-owned enterprises are both part of the ESG problem and part of the potential solution.

The business community in developed and developing countries of course do not speak with a unified voice when it comes to saving the planet from negative climate change and in pursuing good corporate behavior. This is a community with sharply diverse voices and perspectives about how workers should be treated in the twenty-first century, the origins of the climate catastrophe, and its impact. In conversations with climate skeptics, many of whom reside in the corporate sector, I am often struck by their naivete and lack of interest in understanding climate change. Their dismissive talking point is often about today's relatively benign weather, wherever it happens to be, as proof that global warming is either faked or hyped up. In emerging markets, business leaders also tend to underplay the two other pillars of ESG – social and governance, where the emphasis is on treating employees and customers fairly and in ensuring that the company is governed by strong internal rules, processes, and Board oversight.

My own claim to infamy in the ESG field stems from my time at the International Monetary Fund, where I witnessed first-hand how much power is vested with multilateral institutions in shaping our economic future, and most recently at a large international bank where I ran what is confusingly referred to as sustainability – a catch-all phrase meant to explain how the institution is playing its part in being more sustainable and in building pathways away from an entrenched portfolio of carbon-intensive activities.

The challenge I have figured out is in the framing and the question must be asked early and urgently – is ESG a massive virtue-signaling operation where business is embracing the narrative to do good but tangible evidence of real progress is hard to come by? The evidence is unsurprisingly mixed. By the yardstick of talking the talk, the corporate sector in America is certainly not shying away. Data research firm Fact Set searched for the term "ESG" in the conference call transcripts of all the S&P 500 companies that conducted earnings conference calls between December 2021 and April 2022.[5] "Of these companies, 155 cited the term 'ESG' during their earnings calls" Fact Set notes "This number marked the highest overall number of S & P 500 companies citing 'ESG' on earnings calls going back at least ten years." Fact Set analysts also dug deeper by analyzing the longer-term ESG track record of the 155 companies. Their conclusion: "Based on Q4 2021, it would appear that companies that are making more progress on their ESG initiatives and scoring higher of ESG ratings may be prone to discuss their ESG initiatives and their progress during their earnings calls." This still begs the question – what about the majority of companies listed on the S & P 500, which are *not* mentioning ESG in their earnings calls? Are these companies content with their existing strategies which underplays the value of ESG considerations in operating a large, complex industrial enterprise? Or are the CEOs of these storied corporations outright ESG or climate deniers, stymying progress for the corporate sector as a whole?

To answer these questions, one must understand the power dynamics of business in America and Europe, which are radically different from that of emerging markets. Vast swathes of business in the developed world in America and even in Europe, a continent traditionally reliant on bank lending, is owned by shareholders, not of the mom and pop variety, but by a very small group of large institutional investors. This elite group comprises giant pension

---

[5]Fact Set Insight Commentary – Do S & P Companies That Discuss "ESG" on Earnings Calls Have Higher ESG ratings? April 18, 2022.

funds, asset managers, sovereign wealth funds, private equity funds, and family offices owned by billionaires. In the US alone, over 80% of the market capitalization of the broad Russell 3000 index is owned by these large institutions, and around 80% of the large cap S&P 500 index.[6] In dollars, this works out to $21.7 trillion and $18 trillion respectively, a staggering amount which in a nutshell showcases the vast power vested in this group of institutional investors. The institutional investors are not necessarily all American, although they tend to dominate the pack. In Europe, large asset managers and insurers like Abrdn, Axa, Allianz, and Norway's pension fund are significant investors with the clout to influence corporate behavior. This elite group of institutional investors would be incomplete without name-checking giant sovereign wealth funds such as Singapore's GIC and Temasek, Saudi Arabia's Public Investment Fund, Abu Dhabi's Mubadala, and the Qatar Investment Authority.

In this small group, no one looms larger than Larry Fink and BlackRock. For the uninitiated, BlackRock is the world's largest asset manager with a phenomenal $10 trillion in assets under management. It's investment reach extends far and wide into the developed and developing world. When Larry Fink, the all-powerful CEO of BlackRock picks up the phone and calls one of the CEOs of the vast companies in his portfolio, he is never placed on hold or asked to leave a message. The CEO on the other side of the line quivers, and I have witnessed this first-hand, and is often anxious to reassure Fink that all is well on his patch and no nasty surprises await. When Fink or one of his top lieutenants come calling in person, companies bring out the finest silver and their shiniest investor deck to showcase performance. Although the corporate sector in Europe, Japan, and emerging markets are less reliant on equity markets and more on traditional bank lending, global-minded companies still bow to BlackRock because of the firm's sheer convening power in arranging capital. The 345-odd companies in the S&P 500 not citing ESG in their earning calls better watch out.

---

[6]The 2017 data cited above is from Pension & Investments.

Using geopolitical phraseology, BlackRock is the unquestioned investment superpower and Fink is a combination of Henry Kissinger, Metternich, Machiavelli, and even the Pope – the *uber* power broker, diplomat, and ideologue of our age who dispenses homespun wisdom and advice on what CEOs and companies under BlackRock's stewardship should do and should not do in terms of improving performance and overall do-goodery. One of the more remarkable developments over the past decade has been Fink and BlackRock's unconditional embrace of ESG as an organizing principle. In late January each year, and I exaggerate (only a little bit), the most eagerly awaited event for CEOs of BlackRock's portfolio companies is the arrival of the "annual letter" from Fink, equivalent to the encyclical issued by the Pope on weighty spiritual and societal matters. Fink's penmanship and prestige has not yet reached the Pope's or Warren Buffet levels,[7] but the BlackRock CEO has used his powerful platform to persuade, influence, and cajole portfolio companies to place ESG as the fundamental operating principle in managing their business. Here is a classic sampler of Finkese from his 2020 letter to CEOs,[8] which emphasized the importance of climate action and sustainability. "We believe that all investors, along with regulators, insurers, and the public, need a clearer picture of how companies are managing sustainability-related questions" Fink wrote "The data should extend beyond climate to questions around how each company serves its full set of stakeholders, such as the diversity of its workforce, the sustainability of its supply chain, or how well it protects its customer data. Each company's prospects for growth are inextricably linked from its ability to operate sustainably and serve its full set of stakeholders." Lest the recipients of the Fink letter were tempted to ignore or side-step his advice, Fink had the following to say in bold. "Given the groundwork we have already laid engaging on disclosure, and the growing investment risks surrounding sustainability, we will be increasingly disposed to vote against management and board directors when companies are not

---

[7]Buffet, known as the "sage of Omaha," attracts a huge investor following globally. They all converge to his annual shareholder meeting like devotees to a religious cult.
[8]Larry Fink's 2020 Letter to CEOs – A fundamental reshaping of finance.

making sufficient progress on sustainability-related disclosures and the business practices and plans underlying them."

Fink's warning about the risks of corporate inaction notwithstanding, there are prominent segments of business in America and Europe who are either misreading or ignoring his message altogether. Take global banking heavyweight HSBC as a recent example where there is a disconnect in the rhetoric at the highest levels of the bank. HSBC's website makes the bold proclamation that the bank is committed to a "sustainable future" and dedicating between $750 billion and $1 trillion to help clients on this journey. "We are setting out an ambitious plan to prioritise financing and investment that supports the transition to a net zero global economy – and helps to build a thriving resilient future for society and businesses," the bank declares. Stuart Kirk, a senior bank official who was the Global Head for Responsible Investing, did not get the memo or chose to subvert the institution's climate agenda. Speaking at a "Moral Money" event organized by the *Financial Times*,[9] Kirk let loose by noting that in his 25-year banking career, "there was always some nut-job telling me about the end of the world," likening the climate crisis to Y2K which fueled fears about a widespread computer glitch at the turn of the millennium. "Unsubstantiated, shrill, partisan self-serving, apocalyptic warnings are ALWAYS wrong," Kirk wrote in the slide presentation. To be sure, comparing the climate crisis (which is truly apocalyptic based on current trends) with the Y2K kerfuffle (which threatened to temporarily disrupt our online world) is ridiculous, but Kirk's fulminations illustrate a much bigger problem – a sizable section of the business community are ESG and climate deniers, or, like Kirk seemingly underplays the importance of the two.[10]

Even in grey London, where the talk about today's weather is the most popular icebreaker with strangers and acquaintances, Kirk is not alone. There is a formidable group of City grandees, bankers, traders, and assorted asset management types who are either climate skeptics or outright climate deniers. In the run-up to the

---

[9]HSBC Banker attacks climate "hyperbole," *Financial Times*, May 22, 2022.
[10]To be sure, Kirk's employer has reaffirmed its commitment to combating climate change and has placed him under suspension.

2016 Brexit referendum, I was forced to attend a meeting of City worthies to discuss funding for an education initiative in the Commonwealth, a great passion of the British ruling class, forever nostalgic about empire and the bygone imperial era gone by. The group was predominantly white, male and in their sixties, fortified by years of privilege, fine wine, holidays in France, and not having to explain their rather outdated views. On the surface, this was a worldly wise group, many of the participants ran global functions, had traveled extensively, and were sophisticated in their under-standing of how the world works. Or at least I thought. My spell was broken when one participant, a young lady in her thirties, innocently suggested climate education as a worthy cause to sup-port under the Commonwealth initiative. The reaction from the elderly grandees was swift and ruthless. The young interloper was accused of mixing up her facts and bringing "fake" ideas to the table. There was chilly silence in the room after the grandees spoke up and the young lady later told me that he felt like she was gazing at the disembodied eye of Sauron (from the *Lord of the Rings* trilogy), so fearful was the gaze of participants around the table.

I feel the same chill from climate deniers when I navigate the corridors of Washington D.C., where they have thrived for decades – before, during, and well after the Trump era. Unlike City gran-dees, who are suspicious about the science behind climate change, their counterparts in D.C. are skeptics and deniers mainly for profit and wealth accumulation. I don't seriously expect the oil industry lobbyist advocating for greater shale licenses to be a climate skeptic. However, just as the capital city he thrives in, the lobbyist can silence any serious discussion about climate change with what-aboutery, obfuscation, and obstruction. A favored talking point is that the jury is still out on global warming, i.e., there are many scientists who are unconvinced about the speed of acceleration and the lobbying industry prospers by bringing unaccredited scientists to Capitol Hill to argue this case. Oil major Exxon Mobil was the godfather of climate deniers, using the American Petroleum Insti-tute in D.C. as the primary platform to rebut the fundamental role that oil majors play in damaging the environment. Indeed, it came to light a few years ago that Exxon and its peer companies had been aware as early as the 1970s about the oil-induced impact of climate change. This was also the period when oil companies reaped astonishing profits from their fossil fuel franchise, and it is perhaps understandable that they sought to defend their turf from climate activists and do-gooders. It is divine justice that the curiously named Engine No 1, a hedge fund with ESG objectives ran a successful shareholder proxy campaign in 2021 and has been able to install three Director's on the oil major's Board. Supporting Engine No 1 in this high-profile proxy battle was none other than Black-Rock, another Exxon shareholder along with a few of its peers.

The broader point is that if major power centers like London and Washington D.C. are business epicenters of climate lobbying and denial, what possible hope is there for developing countries where politics is more febrile and subject to state capture by the business community? The answer, as I will explore in subsequent chapters, will be through a combination of enlightened governments, citizenry, and the business community joining forces to deal with the most profound challenge of our lifetimes. The challenge is existential, and there is bound to be serious opposition, as we are already witnessing, in making tangible progress in reducing the pace of increase in global temperatures and in compliance with ESG principles.

While Larry Fink and his firm's climate and ESG advocacy are necessary, there are other vastly more powerful societal forces that have successfully been holding business to account for their misbehaviors and acts of omission. By the yardstick of sheer bravado and *chutzpah*, international NGO Greenpeace stands out as an activist group which is willing to go the extra mile to hold companies to account. During my stint at Standard Chartered, I was at the receiving end of Greenpeace's polite entreaties, at the start of their campaign on a particular topic, which gradually transformed into a more public and assertive campaign to demand change. The contentious subject at hand was international bank financing of palm oil plantations in South East Asia, which by overwhelming evidence was leading to massive deforestation on the Indonesian side of Borneo. Palm oil barons, among the richest business families in Indonesia and Malaysia, were also *laissez faire* about labor practices. In one case, it came to light that workers on a palm oil plantation had to surrender their identity documents to the company, raising uncomfortable questions about indentured labor practices. Greenpeace came into this campaign fully equipped to deal with a powerful group of international banks. They assembled the evidence from the ground on disastrous end-of-season slash-and-burn practices by palm oil plantations, which has triggered massive forest fires, devastating wildlife and choking many parts of the region in a polluting haze. The negative health impacts have been well documented by Greenpeace and public health experts in the region, yet palm oil barons have proceeded with impunity.

As an NGO with a successful track record of campaigns, Greenpeace has its own Larry Fink, to cajole and persuade corporate titans to change course. Their methods of course are radically different, as I discovered in my own interactions with former Greenpeace International CEOs Kumi Naidoo and Jennifer Morgan. Kumi is a well-known South African activist who has had a chequered career in global civil society. Jennifer is currently Germany's special envoy for international climate action, a remarkable appointment for someone who was not a German citizen when she was appointed[11] and spent years battling with governments and business from the other side of the table.

Greenpeace has a long history in running high-profile environmental campaigns which attract global attention. In June 2011, Kumi himself shot to international prominence by getting arrested in Greenland for boarding an oil rig despite a court injunction. "In dramatic scenes 120km off the west coast of Greenland, Naidoo and another activist boarded the 52,000 tonne Leiv Eiriksson semi-submersible rig, chartered by Scottish oil company Cairn Energy, around 6.45 am on Friday. They climbed 80 ft up one of the rig's legs despite the crew using water cannons to repel them,"[12] The Guardian reported. Naidoo himself told the newspaper that he was calling on Cairn to halt drilling for oil. "For me this is one of the defining environmental battles of our age, it's a fight for sanity

---

[11]Morgan has since obtained German citizenship.
[12]From The Guardian report – June 17, 2011 – Greenpeace head Kumi Naidoo arrested over oil rig protest.

against the madness of a mindset that sees the melting of the Arctic sea as a good thing."

Despite not having $10 trillion in assets under management and funded entirely by membership contributions, Greenpeace was still able to persuade Cairn Energy to abandon the project (although the company claimed that the decision was based on a failure to find meaningful deposits of oil or gas). The NGO uses levers as powerful as money – a well-tested strategy for driving public attention and causing reputation damage of target companies, in order to drive change. Few companies want to place themselves in the uncomfortable position of having to contend with a public campaign which names and shames them. In the case of the palm oil campaign which I cited earlier, discussions between the bank and Greenpeace were initially inconclusive. The NGO responded by sending activists to bank headquarters in Hong Kong and London, distributing pamphlets to staff on the damage caused by palm oil plantations in South East Asia, which the bank was facilitating. To drive home the point about the damage, the NGO also used an inflatable *orang utan*, the adorable Indonesian ape species native to Borneo and on the front-line of the destruction.

I will discuss at length in a subsequent chapter about the growing power and influence of young staff in shaping ESG policies and outcomes of their employers. In many ways, the challenge is also inter-generational as the older, climate skeptic generation makes way for a more socially aware millennial class who feel the urgency and the impact in their daily lives. For this generation, ESG is a must-have for business, not an afterthought. Young people look up to climate activist Greta Thunberg as their role model rather than any aging, fat-cat CEO.

To cut to the chase, young staff want to be associated with reputed organizations and any public indication to the contrary is likely to drive them away. No 20 or 30 something wants to be quizzed over drinks by hostile peers. While the average age of the typical CEO skews older, the average age of staff in most organizations tend to be in the thirties. Author and investor Vivek Ramaswamy, whose political views tend to be on the conservative side, draws a link between tattered corporate reputations in the aftermath of the 2008 financial crisis and the desire of business to restore their image, which coincided with younger employees' hunger to find a higher purpose in their workplaces. "Companies. . .seized on that opportunity to teach this generation that the way to fill that hunger is to go to Ben & Jerry's and order an ice cream with a cup of morality on the side," he said.[13] Ramaswamy added that the danger for this kind of corporate activism is that a "small group of effective corporate elites" begin to "decide what's right for society at large." But companies may not have a choice when their employees are telling them to behave in a certain way. The May 2020 protests in America over the killing of George Floyd, which unleashed a wave of protests across the developed world, was a wake-up call for companies to speak up about deep racial divides and a commitment to improve diversity and inclusion in their own operations.

The generational divide and societal disconnect is a huge opportunity for an NGO such as Greenpeace. This is because its public campaign strategy allows it to appeal directly to the hearts and minds of young staff in large corporate behemoths. In the case of palm oil, the bank publicly announced that it would withdraw financing from the sector altogether. These victories have emboldened Greenpeace and its cohort of activist NGOs to become more assertive in their advocacy and campaigns. In Greenpeace's 2021 strategic plan,[14] the NGO outlines that its global priority "is to dramatically undermine" the fossil fuel sector while it is weak, and while "anger at the system and openness to radical and comprehensive solutions" brought about by COVID-19 remains strong in people's minds and hearts. "The opportunity we see is for Greenpeace across the world and our allies is to remove fossil fuel legitimacy in our societies (and as a result, remove its funding lifeline) by changing narratives and engaging significantly more people in the context of the health of economic crisis and the big plans to 'fix' our economies."

---

[13]The Ramaswamy quote is from The Financial Times – The war on "woke capitalism," May 28, 2022. The Ben & Jerry's reference in the quote is about the ice cream maker's decision in 2021 to stop selling its products in the occupied territories of the West Bank and Gaza.
[14]From Greenpeace – Our Strategic Plan 2021.

While the supply chain shocks from COVID-19 has seriously disrupted the climate transition, ironically making fossil fuels even more essential for near-term global economic stability, the broader point about Greenpeace changing narratives and engaging more people is a powerful one. To put it simply, the general public in developed and developing societies can no longer be counted upon to remain quiescent. In Europe and America, public anger has been building and the 2008 global financial crisis triggered massive protests about bank bailouts and deep inequities in the economic system. In the UK, the Archbishop of Canterbury Justin Welby, a former CFO of an oil company, emerged as the official champion of the Church and an unofficial spokesperson for the general public in advocating for fundamental changes in the incentives and the compensation structure of bankers. "There will always be greed. We are never going to get rid of human nature," the Archbishop told *The Guardian*. "We'd all like more money. I'd like more money…We'd all like that but what is necessary is the inner discipline that says, no, that's not the appropriate way of thinking, behaving, working, living." The Archbishop was framing the contentious issue of banker's pay as a social issue, as in the "S" of ESG, and called upon pay restraint in the financial sector. Banker's pay may not have directly caused the global financial crisis but the distortive compensation structure in the overall corporate sector remains, where in America, for example, CEOs were still paid 351 times as much as a typical worker in 2020.[15] "Exorbitant CEO pay is a major contributor to rising inequality that we could safely do away with" the Economic Policy Institute report said, "CEOs are getting more because of their power to set pay and because so much of their pay (more than 80%) is stock-related, not because they are increasing their productivity or possess specific, high demand skills."

On hindsight the debate about banker's pay might seem to be a marginal issue given the vast accumulation of wealth in the technology sector in the period since the global financial crisis. As I write this, Apple's market capitalization has topped $2.4 trillion

---

[15]CEO pay has skyrocketed 1322% since 1978 – study by Economic Policy Institute, August 20, 2021.

compared with a more sedate $386 billion for JP Morgan, America's largest bank. While the image and reputation of the once-celebrated Silicon Valley founder aka tech bro may have taken a beating, their power and influence remains undiminished. When Elon Musk proclaims ESG to be a "scam," as noted earlier, he is sending a message to his legions of followers that environmental, social, governance is simply "woke" and lacks substance.

What is undeniable is that ESG is a way of getting major corporations to have the inner discipline, which Archbishop Welby has pushed for, to address urgent issues in a fair and transparent manner. The pandemic has accelerated rich-poor divides by allowing educated, more privileged segment of the population, typically in the tech and financial sectors, to work from home, while essential workers on the front-line in dealing with the virus have placed themselves in harm's way. Even for those lucky enough to be able to work from home, there are deep structural problems which remain unaddressed. "Remote workers has introduced massive shifts within the American workforce that are reinforcing pre-existing inequalities" said RAND Corporation staff.[16] "Consider the following examples. The burden of balancing work responsibilities, childcare, virtual schooling, and housework is falling disproportionately on working mothers, leading some observers to argue that the United States is in the midst of a 'she-cession' in which unprecedented rates of women are dropping out of the labour force."

These inequalities are magnified in emerging markets where the ESG regulatory framework and compliance is extremely weak and business owners tend to get away with lax environmental and labor practices. A truly comprehensive ESG framework which is global in scope is pie-in-the-sky thinking, unrealistic and unattainable in the short term.

A quick word about the scope and structure of the book itself. While my dominant focus is to explore the ESG and the climate landscape in developed countries, I will attempt to also place these

---

[16]The RAND blog – Inequality in Opportunity to work from home an underlying condition aggravated by the pandemic – Kathryn Bouskill and Scott Harold, May 14, 2021.

challenges in their proper context in the three regions I am most familiar with – Asia, the Middle East, and Africa. The book is structured into three parts – first, I explore the historical context of why things are the way they are in terms of our seeming inability to deal with the climate crisis, the entrenched profit motive of the private sector and why it is ill-suited to deal with non-financial issues. The second section dives deeper into the environmental, social, governance pillars and how companies are addressing them at the coal face (pun intended). The final section examines what would it take to make our planet great again – in terms of a fraying social compact between the ruler and ruled at a time of deglobalization, youth activism on ESG issues, and rules of the game for a "new" renewed capitalism. Let's move to the next chapter where we explore the brief history of grime.

2

A BRIEF HISTORY OF GRIME

Behind Every Country's Great Fortune, There Is Grime.

Every story about America should start with a road trip.

The notion of hackers, Russian or otherwise, being committed to climate change is absurd. However, this is precisely what appears to have happened in May 2021 when a group of hackers, supposedly of Russian provenance, disrupted petroleum supplies on the eastern seaboard of the United States. Summers are the peak driving season in America, even one severely disrupted by a global pandemic, and I was ensconced in Myrtle Beach, South Carolina for a wedding when the hackers struck. The target was the operations of Colonial Pipeline, in what is known in the trade as a ransomware cyber-attack. The drive from South California into the Washington, DC, suburbs was about to become challenging.

The little-known Colonial operates the pipeline which supplies petroleum products for much of the eastern United States. Within days of the hacking, the impact of their actions, which in effect locked out the company from its own computer systems, reverberated across the world's largest economy. America runs on many things (including Dunkin Donuts, if the ad is to be believed) but it is the estimated 124 billion gallons of finished motor gasoline consumed in 2020 which graphically explains the country's addiction to four-wheel transportation and the attendant destruction of the planet.

By the time I returned to the Washington DC suburbs where I live, a full-blown panic had set in. In scenes reminiscent of the early 1970s, an issue we will turn to shortly, gas stations all over my neighborhood shuttered operations because of a lack of fuel. A few outlets which were open saw mile-long queues of motorists patiently waiting for their fix of 87, 90, or 94 grade octane fuel. The gas station owner, usually anodyne and anonymous for most customers, briefly experienced a surge in visibility and influence. He cajoled motorists to stay in line and rationed supplies. We were allowed to buy $20 worth of fuel for each car while rumor had it that a neighboring station was allowing a higher $30 allocation.

Like drug addicts in search of our next high, the week of May 10 will be remembered as a time when a new generation of Americans came to the rather glum realization that their entire way of life, powered and made possible by the refined version of thick, oily stuff seeping from the ground, was in jeopardy. It could also have been a teachable moment about our perilous addiction to fossil fuels and the damage it is causing to the planet. However, such self-doubt and reflection barely lasted a nano second as the management of Colonial Pipeline, in their infinite wisdom, decided to pay ransom money to the hackers, believed to be to the tune of 75 bitcoin or $4.4 million. Within a matter of hours, the hackers returned the operating keys to Colonial and the old familiar America came to life again - of permanent gridlock on urban streets and deadly emissions from the tailpipe of cars and trucks.

The hackers were perhaps disappointed with the outcome and next targeted another iconic American firm, JBS Meat for a ransomware attack. Brazilian-owned JBS is not an oil distributor but the world's largest producer of beef, chicken, and pork. The hacking had a similar impact in shutting down production of meat-based protein all over the United States, leading to a scramble in supermarket aisles for storied food products like pork chops and beef tenderloin. As a result, the US Department of Agriculture was unable to offer indicative prices for beef and pork on June 1. In the stodgy but massive business that is food processing, the ransomware attack was a seismic event. In a matter of weeks, a group of unknown hackers had briefly captured control over the supply of a primary fuel, gasoline and essential protein, beef and they were literally laughing all the way to the nearest crypto exchange to mint their proceeds (the JBS ransom pay-out was \$11 million, also in bitcoin).

My speculation on whether the hackers were socially committed rests on the following simple assumption – they targeted fossil fuels which power modern transportation and the farm factories which produce beef. These happen to be two of the world's biggest emitters of greenhouse gases, in the form of toxic carbon dioxide (CO_2) and the lesser well-known methane (CH4), the latter being no laughing matter since it is generated both by leakages from the production of natural gas as well the massive flatulence of cow herds in factory farms. By suspending production of fuel and beef, the hackers were instrumental for reducing CO_2 and CH_4 emissions that week, providing an all too brief respite for a planet which is on the cusp of warming to unsustainable levels. If unchecked, these temperatures could rise to over 1.5 degrees or even 2 degrees above pre-industrial levels according to the Climate Action Tracker.

The skeptics will wonder if a few degrees increase in global temperatures really matter. They need to open their windows and check their basements. As we are discovering through an unprecedented wave of natural disasters – massive forest fires in America and Australia, dangerous flooding in China, Pakistan, and India – global warming or climate change is not a scientific abstraction. It is here in our neighborhood as we sweat, choke, drown, and die in alarmingly large numbers.

Researchers have even quantified the human impact of the planetary devastation – they estimate that "extraordinarily hot and cold temperatures"[1] that are becoming more common as climate change accelerates are responsible for 5 million deaths globally every year. By way of context, an estimated 1.3 million people die globally each year due to road accidents, which until recently was considered a high benchmark to compare mortality statistics. Even COVID-19, a global pandemic like no other has claimed over 20 million lives over a three-year period. With 5 million deaths

---

[1]Climate Change Linked to 5 million deaths a year, new study shows – Bloomberg, July 8, 2021.

expected annually due to global climate change, the world is poised to remain in a permanent state of pandemic.

Researchers from Monash University in Australia and China's Shandong University estimated that there were 74 excess deaths from abnormally cold or hot temperatures for every 100,000 people. Europe had the highest excess death rates per 100,000 people due to heat exposure, Sub-Saharan Africa registered the highest death rates per 100,000 people due to exposure to cold. The largest decline in net mortality, crudely put deaths minus births, happened in Southeast Asia. If this grim data is not a wake-up call, what will be?

Conventional wisdom has it that the pandemic has perversely played a positive role in curbing global warming. This is mistaking the cause for the overall effect. While it is true that major urban centers have witnessed a sharp increase in air quality because the prolonged lockdown of 2020 essentially shut down ground transportation and industrial activity. The fact is that this temporary halt in man-made emissions magically led to blue skies over Mumbai and Beijing is missing the point. The World Meteorological Organization (WMO) explained recently[2] that greenhouse gas concentrations are the cumulative result of past and present emissions of a range of substances, including CO_2, CH_4, and nitrous oxide. Although carbon emissions fell sharply by 17% in 2020 due to the lockdown, the WMO points out that CO_2 levels surged above 410 parts per million (ppm) in 2019 and the "overall effect" of a fall in concentrations in the following year was very small. It is probably going to take a spectacular, sustained reduction in industrial activity over a prolonged period, the decarbonization which experts refer to, to meaningfully move the needle in constraining the rise of temperatures.

The prognosis does not look good. The Intergovernmental Panel on Climate Change (IPCC), which brings together climate science experts to offer an independent, scientific assessment of where we are on global warming, did not mince its words in its sixth assessment issued in the summer of 2021, and in subsequent

---

[2]Climate Change: Covid-19 has little impact on rise of CO_2 – BBC News, November 23, 2020.

reports. "This report is a reality check," said IPCC co-chair Valerie Masson-Delmotte. "We now have a much clearer picture of the past, present, and future climate, which is essential to understanding where we are headed, what can be done, and how we can prepare." The key factoid, which alarmed policy makers, came in the form of a rather bland paragraph in the press release. The report shows that emissions of greenhouse gases are responsible for approximately 1.1 °C of warming since 1850–1900, and finds that averaged over the next 20 years, global temperature is expected to reach or exceed 1.5 °C of warming. It went on to explain that in the coming decades, climate change will increase in all regions. "For 1.5°C of global warming, there will be increasing heat waves, longer warm seasons, and shorter cold seasons. At 2°C of global warming, heat extremes would more often reach critical tolerance thresholds for agriculture and health, the report shows."

Heat extremes and a lack of precipitation are already placing many regions in the world under climate stress. I was in pristine northern California recently, well north of Silicon Valley, and witnessed the impact of a prolonged drought on thousands upon thousands of acres of forest and agriculture land, laid waste from the previous year's fires (perversely followed by record rainfall in 2023). On Route 101 slicing through Sonoma wine country, there are ominous but helpful signs warning motorists about the intensity of a prospective fire hazard – color-coded, and categorized into low, moderate, high, and extreme.

Modern fire-fighting technology has not kept pace with the intensity of the fires in recent years. In Australia, where annual forest fires are predictable, fire fighters have had to deal with an unusual weather phenomenon, where the fires grow so intense that it spawns "fire clouds" which can "generate thunder, lightning, and tornado-force winds," as well as belch out embers – all of which can help spread already fast-moving fires.[3] To return to the IPCC report, it is not just ground temperatures that climate change is impacting.

---

[3]"Fire Clouds": After Australia, scientists warn the erratic weather phenomenon could become a new reality – NBC News, January 14, 2020.

The IPCC report drives home the point that climate change is bringing "multiple different changes" to different regions – which will all increase with further warming. These include intensification of the water cycle, which will bring more intense rainfall and associated flooding; climate change is affecting rainfall patterns, bringing more precipitation in higher altitudes (as happened in Greenland for the first time recently) and a shortfall in lower altitudes, where a majority of the global population resides; intensification in coastal area flooding; an amplification of permafrost thawing and loss of seasonal snow cover; and fundamental changes to how the ocean operates; While I have highlighted the impact of global climate change in stressed areas like California and Australia, the fact remains that a significant cost from the failure of climate mitigation and adaptation will be borne by the world's poor. To date, all that the international community has offered to middle and low-income nations by way of assistance are platitudes, puffery, and pontification. The frequency of statements issued by world leaders and heads of multilateral organizations such as the UN and the IMF, without transparent funding and policy advice, is a clear sign that we may be at the precipice but our leaders sure love to warn us about the obvious without doing much about it. Here is UN Secretary General Antonio Gutteres, a prolific tweeter: "It's time for leaders – public and private alike – to stop talking about renewable energy as a distant project of the future. Without renewables, there can be no future. We don't have a moment to lose." While the Secretary General's intentions are genuine, the fact that the UN with its universal membership has taken hesitant steps in combating climate change is illustrative that advocacy and rhetoric has run its course and the time to act is now.

A shared solution to resolve the climate crisis may therefore lie elsewhere. Perhaps it is in the plucky, global school girl-driven climate protests engineered by Greta Thunberg which could be a force for change. Or it could be with business, the topic of this book, to drive smarter and more effective environmental, social, governance (the notorious ESG of the title). As one of the biggest originators of climate destructive activity, the business community can play a responsible role in steering their activities and the planet onto a more sustainable path.

I do believe in second chances. If we turn the clock back five decades to the early 1970s, the international community had a unique opportunity to reduce its dependence on fossil fuels. It was also a time when corporate power was not as heavily concentrated as it is today and oil companies (even the fabled seven sisters of the era) were briefly brought to their knees. However, many politicians did what they do best – they punted the issue to future generations and the world lost a historic opportunity to place itself on a path of green growth. The inciting incident which I am referring to took place in October 1973 when the Arab members of the Organization of Petroleum Exporting Countries (OPEC), led by Saudi Arabia then as now one of the world's largest oil producers, placed an embargo on oil exports to the United States, then heavily dependent on fossil fuel imports. The historic decision, by a hitherto disunited group of oil exporting Arab nations, was over America's decision to rearm Israel at the height of the Yom Kippur war[4] and to make the impossible possible (using oil as a powerful bargaining chip in geopolitics). The embargo was also extended to nations deemed to be supportive of the US action which included the UK, Canada, the Netherlands, Portugal, and South Africa. "The 1973 Oil Embargo acutely strained a U.S. economy that had grown increasingly dependent on foreign oil" notes the US State Department's official history of this period.[5] "The efforts of President Nixon's administration to end the embargo signaled a complex shift in the global financial balance of power to oil-producing states and triggered a slew of U.S. attempts to address the foreign policy challenges emanating from long-term dependence on foreign oil."

In my view and I will explain this in detail, America and Europe heeded the wrong lessons from the oil embargo. As with the Colonial Oil pipeline shock of 2021, the overwhelming lesson and desire of policymakers, circa 1973, was to restore oil supplies to feed their fossil fuel dependent economies. To reinforce any lessons learned or forgotten, there was a second oil shock in 1979 which was induced by the Iranian Revolution.

---

[4]For the uninitiated, the Yom Kippur war was waged between Israel and Egypt and Syria. The primary objective of Arab nations was to reclaim land ceded to Israel during the previous 1967 conflict.
[5]Oil Embargo 1973–1974, Office of the historian, US Department of State.

For an all-too brief moment during that decade, there was an attempt by consumers to become more environmentally conscious. "These jarring events caused long lines at gasoline stations, introducing American consumers to such rationing measures as 'odd-even' purchases by license plate number, made gas guzzling cars an object of opprobrium and put driving and home-heating costs near the top of household budgets," The New York Times[6] recalled a decade later in 1983. These comments are still relevant in the summer of 2022, when oil prices have returned to three-digit levels following supply disruptions after Russia's invasion of Ukraine. "This is going to be a really big disruption in terms of logistics, and people are going to scramble for barrels," said energy guru Daniel Yergin.[7] "This is a supply crisis, it's a logistics crisis. It's a payment crisis, and this could well be on the scale of the 1970s." However, the 2022 oil shock does not appear to have reduced the average American's proclivity to drive ultra-gas guzzling cars, which remains undiminished. To be sure, America is not the only country where people have gargantuan car appetites. In the oil-rich Gulf, every second vehicle on the streets appears to be the Escalade or the Patrol, SUVs which have no business to be manufactured because of their out-sized consumption and emissions.

Some countries in Europe heeded the lesson from the 1973 oil shock. I recall reading stories from that era in Time and Newsweek magazines documenting how commuters in the Netherlands had decided to take to the bicycle as the more reliable and carbon-neutral mode of transportation. While such awareness appears to have been sticky in the Netherlands, going by the formidable battalion of bicycle riders one encounters in Amsterdam even today, the rest of the developed world was anxious to get back to normal, which meant a return to their addictive, fossil-fuel addled lifestyle.

---

[6]10 Years After Oil Crisis: Lessons Still Uncertain – The New York Times, September 25, 1983.
[7]Yergin is currently Vice Chairman of IHS Markit and author of "The Prize," a seminal history of the global oil industry. The quote is from an interview with CNBC, March 3, 2022

The International Energy Agency,[8] which maintains a historic database of global emissions, estimates that fuel-related emissions were around 15.6 billion metric tons in 1973, around the time of the oil embargo, with oil accounting for over 50% of that. This was substantial for the time but useful to remember that economic activity was heavily concentrated in America and Europe since the two Asian giants China and India and much of the developing world were still asleep at the wheel. In 2021, with better econometric tools at its disposal, the IEA projects[9] that global energy-related emissions remained at 31.5 Gt, "which contributed to CO2 reaching its highest ever average annual concentration in the atmosphere of 412 parts per million (ppm) in 2020 – around 50% higher than when the industrial revolution began." Compared with the 1970s, there has been a substantial, dramatic shift in economic power and activity with China, India, Brazil, and a group of emerging market nations today contributing to a significant share of global GDP. It was in the throes of the second oil shock of 1979 that China under Deng Xiaoping decided to open its moribund economy to trade and investment and in the process the country became one of the largest importers of oil. India followed over a decade later and its own economic journey has similarly been powered by fossil fuel.

In a clear sign of the fatalism which was rampant at the time about oil being the essential, irreplaceable fossil fuel, the Chairman of Exxon was quoted in the same *The New York Times* article as noting that "our industry" is strongly influenced by international events over which "we" have no control. "The unexpected is almost certain to occur and, when it does, efforts by governments to control the consequences can as easily impair or postpone necessary adjustments as facilitate them. We have learned that there are no easy answers." On hindsight, there were easy answers at the time for the world to reflect on and act on. The 1973 oil embargo was a defining moment for America and Europe in altering consumer perceptions about the scarcity and reliability of oil as the essential

---

[8]IEA Charts Rise in Fuel-Related Carbon Emissions – Bloomberg Law, September 2, 2010.
[9]IEA – Global Energy Review 2021.

fuel, but these lessons were soon forgotten. When oil supply was restored, consumers returned to their gas guzzling ways – for their morning commute to work, their summer driving expeditions, and the necessity of having more than one car in the family garage. The world lost a historic opportunity to reset and focus attention on less fuel intensive and polluting alternatives like renewables. While the debate about global warming was still nascent in the early 1970s, it was by no means completely absent from the public narrative.

President Richard Nixon, whose name and Presidency is forever associated and tarnished with the Watergate scandal, was incredibly enough an early supporter of tough environmental legislation. The President's hand was perhaps forced after a devastating oil spill in his home state of California. The January 1969 oil spill, off the pristine shores of Santa Barbara, was the worst ever as an estimated three million gallons of crude oil escaped from a poorly designed well. It was four years before the Arab oil embargo, which heightened global attention on our acute dependence on fossil fuels.

"I remember looking straight down into this huge upwelling of black out of the ocean. And I just instantly thought, this was going to change the world," recalls a student.[10] Richard Nixon had barely been in office for a week into his first term when the oil spill took place. It is easy to imagine a Republican President today, of a particular pedigree and extreme political views, who would have denied the science and the environmental damage wrought by the oil spill. The late 1960s was a different era, which enabled President Nixon to embrace the science and issue the following stirring statement: "What is involved is the use of our resources of the sea and the land in a more effective way and with more concern for preserving the beauty and the natural resources that are so important to any kind of society that we want for the future. The Santa Barbara incident has frankly touched the conscience of the American people," the President said after visiting

---

[10]Paul Relis was a student at the University of California, Santa Barbara and witnessed the spill first-hand. His account appeared as oral history and in the *Smithsonian* magazine – "How an Oil Spill Inspired the First Earth Day," April 22, 2019.

one of the oil-spilt beaches.[11] He declared the 1970s to be the "decade of the environment" by introducing a series of landmark legislation aimed at protecting the environment. This included the creation of the Environment Protection Agency (EPA), a federal agency which President Trump sought to make impotent, and important legislation like the Environmental Policy Act and the Clean Air and Clean Water Acts. The first Earth Day, which is celebrated globally with much fanfare in April each year, was born out of the Santa Barbara oil spill and the robust environmental activism which it generated. For a moment it seemed that the world's largest economy was going to radically break away from its history of grime and chart a bold new green pathway.

Enter Milton Friedman to ensure it never happened. Now acolytes of the late, great Nobel Prize-winning economist will skewer me for blaming one of our greatest economists for destroying the environment. I rest my case on an important article (and subsequent paper) which Friedman authored in September 1970, around 18 months after the Santa Barbara oil spill. To be sure, Friedman's article had little to do with the environment. It was focused squarely on corporate responsibility and what it should be. He established the "Friedman doctrine" which sets out in blunt prose that the primary responsibility of business was to make money for its shareholders and dismissed the notion of that much-abused phrase - corporate social responsibility. Let me get out of the way and allow Friedman to explain in his own words what the primary responsibility of business should be and should not be. "In a free enterprise, private-property system, a corporate executive is an employee of the owners of business. He has direct responsibility to his employers. That responsibility is to conduct the business in accordance with their desires, which generally will be to make as much as money as possible while conforming to the basic rules of the society, both those embodied in law and those embodied in ethical custom," Friedman wrote in a historic essay for *The New York Times*.[12]

---

[11]Richard Nixon's Response to the Santa Barbara Oil Spill – From the Richard Nixon Foundation, July 1, 2010.
[12]A Friedman doctrine – The Social Responsibility of Business is to Increase its Profits – *The New York Times*, September 13, 1970.

To ensure that his message was not lost, he went on to explain that the notion that a corporate executive has a social responsibility is "pure rhetoric": "For example, that he is to act in some way that is not in the interest of his employers. For example, that he is to refrain from increasing the price of the product to contribute to the social objective of preventing inflation, even though a price increase would be in the best interests of the corporation. Or that he is to make expenditures on reducing pollution beyond the amount that is in the best interests of the corporation or that is required by law to contribute to the social objective of improving the environment." He emphasized that "in each of these cases," the corporate executive would be spending "someone else's money" for the general social interest.

The "Friedman doctrine" had far-reaching influence on the attitudes of corporate America. What he was articulating was the purest form of *laissez faire* capitalism and it is no coincidence that the economist was a great admirer of colonial Hong Kong's post-1945 capitalist system where the state stayed away from business and the rules were light.

I must briefly come to Friedman's defense to note that he did not actually advocate for companies to maximize shareholder value at the expense of destroying the environment. His inelegant and incorrect advocacy was for corporations not to break the law but to place profits and shareholders at the expense of everything else, including social impact. Money which companies spent on corporate philanthropy, in his view, was better spent by paying out to shareholders in the form of dividends and then allocated by them by charity. This construct is problematic because no individual shareholder at the time and certainly the case today has the clout and financial muscle of a modern corporation in influencing social outcomes. The "Friedman doctrine" had the intended consequence of originating the idea that "greed is good," which was to be uttered 17 years later by the fictional Gordon Gecko in Oliver Stone's movie Wall Street.

How relevant is the Friedman doctrine for contemporary business, in a world in midst of war and emerging from a pandemic? "Some argue that shareholder interests go beyond money, and that a single focus on profits short-changes these priorities," writes Amy

Merrick in the *Chicago Booth Review*.[13] "Others suggest that a
time when corporations have an out-size role in shaping the regulations that govern them, businesses are inextricable from the
societies in which they operate, and that it's time to develop principles of shared success." Fifty-three years is a long time for a
section of business to arrive at the grudging conclusion that operating a business is much more than profit maximization. In the
interim, the set of corporate beliefs propagated by Friedman and his
acolytes caused maximum damage to the fabric of American society. Failed 1992 Presidential contender Ross Perot, who was also a
billionaire businessman, was prescient when he attacked the North
America Free Trade Agreement (NAFTA) and spoke about the
"giant sucking sound" of American jobs migrating south to Mexico
because of the differential levels of regulation, development, and
wages.

Now I happen to be an ardent supporter of free trade, with
caveats, and believe that the rise of China, India, and Vietnam in
the 1980s and 1990s would not have been possible without
America opening its doors to trade and investment flows. It is no
contradiction that this opening up also represents the single-biggest
failure in American public policy in recent decades. Friedman's
thinking on shareholder value and profit maximization removed
shackles from corporate executives and the financiers on the real
Wall Street. When jobs started leaving America to cheap wage
destinations like Mexico and China, policymakers were still in
thrall with the Friedman doctrine and super CEOs like GE's Jack
Welch, who has been described in a recent book[14] as the man who
"broke" American capitalism. Welch's strategy *du jour* at GE was
relentless cost-cutting and profit maximization, accompanied by
significant pay increases to himself and his management cohort.
"An intellectual revolution had been coursing through academic,
legal, and political circles," David Gelles writes (focused on

---

[13]Is the Friedman Doctrine Still Relevant in the 21st Century? – Amy
Merrick, *Chicago Booth Review*, May 24, 2021.
[14]The Man Who Broke Capitalism: How Jack Welch Gutted the Heartland
and Crushed the Soul of America – and How to Undo His Legacy – by David
Gelles, Simon & Schuster, April 2022. I have also drawn on a review of the
book which appeared in *The New York Times*, June 2, 2022.

corporate downsizing, deal making, and financialization) but "no one had truly put his philosophy to work"... until Welch. As a result, the CEO became the personification of "American alpha-male capitalism."

America's dominant political class in the 1990s happened to be the Democratic Party, with Clinton in the White House and free marketeers like Robert Rubin and Lawrence Summers in senior Treasury positions. One of the administration's signature achievements was gutting of the Depression-era Glass-Steagall Act, which separated risk-prone investment banks from deposit-taking commercial entities as a way to minimize financial stability risks and to the consumer. The dismantling of Glass-Steagall in the 1990s incentivized Wall Street to create mega banks, the creation of Citigroup in 1998 being a notable example, and was the proximate reason for the collapse of the American financial system a decade later. In the profit maximization environment that has thrived in the period before and immediately after, it is no surprise that ESG did not feature as a priority or indeed on the screens of major American CEOs. The American capitalist model were a hot export item to emerging markets like China and India which fashioned their own economic policies built on giving free enterprise free rein.

Turning the clock back is wistful thinking. For a brief moment in the early 1970s, the America, and to great extend the world faced a simple choice – build on Nixon's track record of early environmental legislation or follow Friedman into the land where shareholder was God and corporate profits came before the planet. In my view, the less worthy idea won. "Friedman's theory was wildly popular because it seemed to absolve corporations of difficult moral choices and to protect them from public criticism as long as they made profits," writes Eric Posner.[15] From the ashes of the 1973 oil embargo, came the carbon-industrial complex and the world today defined by Milton Friedman, which we will turn to in the next chapter.

---

[15]Milton Friedman was Wrong – Eric Posner, *The Atlantic*, August 22, 2019.

3

OUR CARBON-INDUSTRIAL
COMPLEX

The Perverse Economics Behind the Global Economy's Reliance on All Things Carbon.

Ground zero to understanding our heavy dependence on the carbon-dominated economy is to look at the emissions footprint of the largest fighting entity on earth – the US Armed Forces. Watching the latest *Top Gun* movie, where actor Tom Cruise takes to the skies to indulge in astonishing aerial acrobatics under the guise of training, prompts me to ask a rhetorical question: Is anyone at the Pentagon paying attention to the sheer volume of fuel that an F-18 Super Hornet, used in the movie to great effect, will burn through a training exercise in the real world? More importantly, is there anyone at the Pentagon fretting about carbon emissions from the US Armed Forces' massive global footprint?

While the Pentagon's own climate strategy is thin on specifics, which we will come to later, an independent assessment of its carbon footprint has arrived at the following damaging conclusion. "The U.S. Department of Defense is the largest institutional consumer of fossil fuels in the world and a key contributor to climate change," declared a report published by the Watson Institute (affiliated with Brown University) in 2019.[1] "Between 2001 and 2017, the years for which data is available since the beginning of the war on terrorism with the U.S. invasion of Afghanistan, the U.S. military emitted 1.2 billion metric tons of greenhouse gases. More than 400 million tons of greenhouse gases are directly due to war-related fuel consumption. The largest portion of Pentagon fuel consumption is military jets." Which kind of proves my earlier point that grounding Tom Cruise and achieving world peace will be beneficial to the planet. To place the Watson Institute report in perspective, it is useful to look at the real world impact of the Pentagon's hyper emissions. It is equivalent to the annual emissions of 257 million passenger cars, which are double the current number of cars on the roads in America. If the US Armed Forces were a nation, it would be a bigger emitter than entire nations like Portugal, Morocco, Sweden, and Switzerland.

Since the Biden administration is a strong supporter of global efforts to combat climate change, it came as a shock to many that the President's December 2021 executive order,[2] directing the Federal government to reach 100% carbon-free electricity by 2030 and net zero emissions by 2050, offered a generous exemption to "national security, combat, intelligence, or military training." There will be no meaningful reduction in the Federal government's carbon footprint without including the Pentagon, which accounts for a stunning 80% of overall emissions. The strangest aspect of this is that successive heads of the US department of defense and senior generals routinely warn about the global security risks from climate change. Here is the current incumbent Lloyd Austin speaking about the risks from climate change and the need to adapt just two months before Biden signed the executive order. "Climate change is an existential threat to our nation's security, and the Department of Defense must act swiftly and boldly to take on this challenge and prepare for damage that cannot be avoided," he said.[3] The Watson

---

[1]Pentagon Fuel Use, Climate Change, and the Costs of War – report by Watson Institute, June 2019.
[2]Executive Order on Catalyzing Clean Energy Industries and Jobs Through Federal Sustainability – The White House, December 8, 2021.
[3]Statement by Secretary of Defense Lloyd Austin on the Department of Defence Climate Adaptation Plan – October 7, 2021.

Institute is clear on what the Pentagon needs to do. "The U.S. military has an opportunity to reduce risks associated with climate change – and the security threats associated with climate change – by reducing their role in creating greenhouse gas emissions," it noted.

It may be too much of a stretch to expect the Pentagon to commandeer a fleet of electric-powered tanks and jets at short notice (although it is working with the private sector on electric vehicles repurposed for military use). There is no Elon Musk-type figure in the defense establishment demanding or leading the charge in greening the world's most formidable fighting machine. As the Russia-Ukraine conflict illustrates, war is still dirty business, fought with conventional infantry and artillery. The sight of the Russian Army marooned enroute to Kyiv in March 2022 due to shortages of fuel and food illustrates that if the US Armed Forces is behind the curve in grappling with emissions, the prospects for fighting forces elsewhere (China, India, Russia) are progressively worse. The conflict has also had a salutary effect by boosting defense spending in conflict-averse Europe, which has consistently under-spent on military hardware but has been progressive overall on sustainability. Perhaps the EU will lead the way in building an environmentally sustainable Army over the next decade. Much of the global attention on the future of war has focused on high-fangled notions of the machines and AI taking over. While cyber is indeed the new battle frontier, the fact remains that the world will continue to plunge into periodic wars the old-fashioned way and greening is not going to be top priority. In the interim, Austin and his peers will continue to warn about the global risks from climate change but will do very little to address it in their own operations.

The challenges faced by the world's largest fighting force have many parallels with the business world, the focus of this book, where corporate chieftains are eager to talk the talk about sustainability but are nowhere close to walking it. Just as the Pentagon emits out-sized emissions in its daily operations, another independent report[4] published in 2017 estimated that just 100 companies have been the source "of more than 70% of the world's greenhouse gas emissions since 1988." "The report found that more than half of global industrial emissions since 1988 – the year the Intergovernmental Panel on Climate Change was established – can be traced to *just* 25 corporate and state-owned entities. The scale of historical emissions associated with these fossil fuel producers is large enough to have contributed significantly to climate change," reported *The Guardian*.[5] The list of companies includes a rogue's gallery of the fossil fuels sector – they include publicly-listed Exxon Mobil, Chevron, BP, and Shell but also state-owned fossil fuel majors in the developing world – Saudi's Aramco, Coal India, PetroChina, and Gazprom, the source of current European angst over natural gas supplies during the Ukraine conflict.

Before we express collective outrage and threaten to cancel the Pentagon and major fossil fuel producers for their role in destroying the planet, we should look at our own behaviors in aiding and abetting the climate crisis. The carbon-industrial complex is the foundation of the global economy and fossil fuel companies are only one link in a complex climate chain. The Global Carbon Project estimates that between 1750 and 2018, the US alone emitted a phenomenal 397 billion tons of CO_2, followed closely by China (214), Russia (180, including the former Soviet Union), Germany, and the UK (90 and 77 respectively). There is a vast army of enablers, the middle-men, intermediaries, and end-users, who have profited handsomely from the burning of this carbon – the financiers who provide much of the capital, the technologists, and the manufacturers who consume vast amounts of energy to produce goods and services, and at the last mile, the consumer, particularly in the developed world who has a rapacious appetite for cheap made-in-China trinkets, gas guzzling cars, cheap air travel options, and cheaper tourist destinations. The transmission mechanism for climate destruction is through this malign supply chain. Personal

[4]The Carbon Majors report, published by CDP and the Climate Accountability Institute, July 2017. A subsequent report was published by the Carbon Accountability Institute in October 2019.
[5]Just 100 companies responsible for 71% of global emissions, study says – *The Guardian*, July 10, 2017.

responsibility to protect the planet has seldom featured in global climate discussions, which should be a top priority.

In a recent conversation with a friend, currently in a senior role at a firm which requires constant business travel, I was struck by his candor in admitting that he did not "think much" about sustainability in his business and personal life. His work schedule was dotted by long-haul travel, like most corporate warriors. I must admit that although I headed the sustainability function at a major international bank through much of the past decade, I did little to curb my own international travel. They are the skeptics who believe that individual responsibility, while important, is not a major driver in combating global warming. Anders Levermann, a professor at the Potsdam Institute for Climate Impact Research, is amongst the non-believers. "Personal sacrifice alone cannot be the solution to tackling the climate crisis" he writes.[6] "There's no other area in which the individual is held so responsible for what's going wrong. And it's true: people drive too much, eat too much meat, and fly too often." Leversmann added that reaching zero emissions requires very fundamental changes "Individual sacrifice alone will not bring us to zero. It can only be achieved by structural change: by a new industrial revolution."

Such a revolution, in my view, will not be possible without broad public support in developed and developing countries, *with* individuals understanding their personal contribution to saving the planet. There is also much to be said about the structure of the global economy since China's accession to the World Trade Organization (WTO), which opened up the floodgates to the current divisive world order, where trade surplus countries like China, Germany, and others in East Asia became export powerhouses and trade deficit countries, notably America, imported vast quantities of consumer goods to satisfy the appetite of the consumer. For a period of time, the economic compact worked and China became the world's factory. As long as consumers benefited from hyper-low retail prices, enabled by China's hyper-low production costs, the world economy happily chugged along. Few people paid attention

---

[6]Individuals can't solve the climate crisis. Governments needs to step up – Anders Levermann, *The Guardian*, July 10, 2019.

to the horrific environmental and social costs associated with this unholy compact. As China expanded production capacity to satisfy the world market, it also triggered a global commodities super-cycle, the likes of which the world has not seen.[7]

Some relevant data from the World Bank from that period is striking. It shows that China's primary energy consumption during the 2000–2014 period tripled, its share of global oil consumption doubled, and its metal consumption alone accounted for nearly all of the net increase in global consumption during that period. The Indian economy also grew rapidly during this period but its commodity and CO_2 emissions footprint is significantly smaller compared with China. The next time an investment bank proclaims that another commodity super-cycle is upon us, as Goldman Sachs recently advocated,[8] we should ask two fundamental questions. First, what impact will the surging demand have on environmental, social factors in developed and developing countries. Second, the composition of commodity demand should be examined further. If most of it is in fossil fuels, this should be a red flag that global warming is likely to get worse. However, if much of the demand is for "green" metals – copper, lithium, graphite, cobalt, vanadium – it will be a hopeful sign that the global economy is indeed decarbonizing. "Green" metals are of course are a misnomer since they come with their own ESG costs which we will discuss in a subsequent chapter. My general point is that we cannot absolve individual consumers from their behaviors which has played a major role in climate distress.

The pandemic has of course been transformative in reshaping individual and corporate behaviors, in changing attitudes toward remote working and less business travel in favor of Zoom calls. In the broad scheme of things, these changes in attitudes are superficial because they do not address the challenges required for businesses to decarbonize. The fundamental distortions and perversions in our

---

[7]The World Bank notes that the surge in commodity prices in the 2000s as the fourth "super cycle" in the last 150 years. See On booms and super-cycles: China and India's central role in global commodity markets, July 31, 2015.
[8]Goldman proclaims the dawn of a new commodity super cycle – *Reuters*, January 5, 2021.

carbon economy, with fossil fuels once again playing a dominant role, continue apace as the recent conflict in Ukraine has amply demonstrated.

Oil and gas prices have risen sharply due to Russia's invasion of Ukraine, a result of supply dislocations and an increase in demand in a recovering global economy from the pandemic. Conventional thinking about fossil fuels and major oil companies during the pandemic amounted to the following. Investors and banks should withdraw from supporting fossil fuel industries because it was inevitably headed in the direction of the dinosaur. "Not only is it morally risky, it's economically risky," said Micheal Brune,[9] executive director of the Sierra Club, one of America's major environmental advocacy groups, "The world is moving away from fossil fuels toward clean energy and is doing so at an accelerated pace. Those left holding investments in fossil fuel companies will find their investments becoming more and more risky over time."

Michael Brune's comments are reflective of a more hopeful era, after the pandemic and before Russia's invasion of Ukraine. It was a short-lived moment when energy transition became the guiding principle, with the widespread belief that fossil fuels would soon become history. The peak moment for energy transition advocates was surely the COP26 climate summit at Glasgow, where oil and gas companies were shut out of the proceedings altogether. "We are not villains in this case" huffed Tengku Mohammed Taufik, chief executive of Petronas, Malaysia's national oil company "We are part of the solution." This show-stopper was preceded with the incoming Biden administration's refusal (when it assumed power in January 2021) to engage officially with Saudi Arabia's Crown Prince Mohammed Bin Salman, or MBS for short (over his alleged involvement in the Istanbul killing of journalist Jamal Khashoggi), with the President himself describing the Crown Prince as a "pariah."

However, geopolitics has a charming way of upending conventional wisdom and the strongest of political principles. "At COP26, nobody wanted to see us," said Felipe Bayon, chief executive of Ecopetrol, "In four or five months, the conversations has shifted

---

[9]Brune was quoted in same Guardian article cited earlier.

dramatically because of geopolitics. How can we play a different role as an industry and lead that transformation."[10] Since COP26 concluded in November 2021, supply chain dislocations from the pandemic and the Russian invasion created unprecedented shortages of oil and natural gas, sending crude oil prices above $100 a barrel and natural gas imported into Europe to record levels. As high oil and gas prices created real pain to the American and European consumer, the Biden administration was forced to backtrack on its policy and pleaded with Saudi Arabia, as the world's largest oil producer, to increase supply and moderate prices. The pleas were also directed at American oil majors to step up supply, with Exxon reaping windfall profits of $56 billion, up from $23 billion in the previous year. Not bad for an oil major which was dismissed as a relic by energy transition advocates and fought a losing battle with an activist investor, Engine No 1, who only owned 0.02% of the company but managed to secure two Board seats at a contentious shareholder's meeting in 2021. "The fund's arguments were strategic rather than ideological: that the company's returns have been consistently disappointing shareholders over the last 10 years, and that it needed fresh direction in a rapidly decarbonising world," writes Samanth Subramaniam in *Quartz*.[11] To rub salt into Exxon's wounds, supporting Engine No 1 in its activism was none other than BlackRock which voted against Exxon's leadership along with a group of influential institutional investors. BlackRock on its part has defended its continued strategy of owning fossil fuel stocks in its portfolio, creating the unfortunate impression of wanting its fossil fuel cake and advocating otherwise too.

These contradictions highlight America's own role as a major oil and gas producer which conflict at times with its commitment to take the lead in the fight against climate change. How can the US possibly ask oil and gas producers to step up production, as it did in the spring of 2022, to deal with a sharp spike in prices while simultaneously attempt to curb emissions and limit the increase in

[10]The quotes from Bayon and Taufik are taken from the energy news portal Upstream, March 10, 2022 and March 8, 2022.
[11]Engine No. 1: The little hedge fund that shook Big Oil – Quartz, May 28, 2021.

global temperatures? To put it simply, this square cannot be circled. The role of natural gas as the so-called "bridge fuel," i.e., serving as a bridge in the world's transition from pure fossil fuels into renewables is yet another contentious issue. One "wrinkle" in the bridge-fuel argument, as a recent article in The New York Times[12] put it, is unburned methane which is emitted from the production process. *During the first twenty years after its release, it is more than 80 times as powerful as carbon dioxide at warming the climate* (italics mine). "You don't have to be a chemistry professor to understand the conundrum," The Times article noted, "If you can get the gas out of the ground and into a power plant without letting it leak, it releases less carbon or oil. If you let too much of it escape into the atmosphere while producing it, though, you might damage the climate more than if you just left it in the ground and burned coal instead." Methane leaks from natural gas pipelines are fairly routine.

These contradictions are not just an American issue. After positioning itself as a progressive, pro-green advocate, the European Commission (the administrative arm of the European Union) raised hackles by labeling natural gas and nuclear power as being a green and sustainable fuel. The European Commission's Financial Services chief's conceded that the proposal was "imperfect." "However, I believe that we have found a balance between fundamentally different opinions," Commissioner Mairead McGuiness said,[13] in reference to fierce lobbying on both sides of the proposition, "The end is a low-carbon future powered by renewable energy. We do not have the capacity for that yet."

The Commissioner is absolutely right in noting that the world is not fully ready to switch to renewable energy as yet. We are therefore doomed to remain in this energy transition limbo – where renewable energy's share of a country's fuel mix is increasing but not fast enough to ensure an early transition. Some relevant data from the Centre for Climate and Energy Solutions (C2ES)[14] makes

---

[12]How One Restaurateur Transformed America's Energy Industry – The New York Times, July 6, 2022.
[13]Europe's plan to call natural gas "sustainable" triggers backlash from climate campaigners – CNN Business, February 2, 2022.
[14]Renewable Energy – Note by C2ES.

for encouraging reading. Renewable energy is the fastest growing energy source in the United States, increasing 42% from 2010 to 2020, currently accounting for around 20% of utility-scale US electricity generation in 2020. Globally, renewables made up 29% of electricity generation in 2020, much of it from hydropower. Making the leap from 29% of global electricity generation to a dominant 60–70% by the end of the decade is the profound challenge of our generation. So is increasing the share of electric vehicles on the streets of the world's major cities. Estimates suggest that nearly 10% of all cars sold worldwide in 2021 were electric – around 6 million of the 66.7 million total cars sold during the year. The obstacles are daunting to get to full electrification of the global car fleet, not least because of the ubiquitous charging infrastructure required to keep drivers from developing range anxiety. Electrification of mobility is a good story which financial markets seem to love. How else can one explain Tesla's disproportionately large market capitalization ($728 billion at its peak) compared with its much bigger conventional combustion engine rivals like Toyota ($255 billion)? The difference between the two can be explained away as the premium which the world is prepared to reward a fully electric carmaker. But the devil will be in the details of governments getting the incentive structure right – in striking the right balance between reducing dependence on fossil fuels and aggressively building the green infrastructure to ensure a smooth transition.

In this context, an early phase out of natural gas by Europe, made necessary because of the continent's reliance on imports from Russia, now increasingly looks like a pipe dream. "This will delay a desperately needed real sustainable transition and deepen our dependency on Russian fuels," said Greta Thunberg, "The hypocrisy is striking, not surprising." The EU proposal referenced earlier has since been approved by the European Parliament and the rules will go into effect in 2023. The EU has pledged to cut emissions by 55% from 1990 levels by 2030 and become a net-zero emissions economy by 2050. These ambitious goals look tenuous as the EU's urgent focus in the aftermath of the Russian invasion is energy security (i.e., oil and gas) rather than securing a green transition.

Due to the prolonged pandemic, fossil fuels have also returned to favor in China, which had declared an ambitious goal of achieving net zero by 2060 and to scale up renewable energy's contributions to the national grid. China's energy dilemma illustrates a fundamental disconnect in the global climate discourse – rhetoric is racing ahead of actual delivery of commitments. Any credible energy transition will have to factor in the role of fossil fuels in the energy mix for the foreseeable future, albeit on a declining slope. China faced severe electricity shortages in the last quarter of 2021, unusual for a country which has built up formidable energy infrastructure. Although renewable energy has made impressive strides in recent years, the "dirty secret" is that China still runs on coal.[15] It accounted for 56.8% of the nation's power supply in 2020 and has remained steady throughout the last few years. There are also signs that China is backing away from its global climate commitments for two reasons. First, as outlined earlier, the protracted energy squeeze has led to a rethink in its plans to shutter coal production. Second, the geopolitical environment has transformed with China pitted in a battle for global supremacy against America, which is unfolding at an early stage. China may calculate that no geopolitical advantage is to be gained if it pushes ahead with bold decarbonization plans, while climate plans of its principal rival is mired in domestic politics and dysfunction.

The overarching lesson here is that when governments lead on climate change, citizens and business are likely to follow. When governments dither, as many of them routinely do in their climate pronouncements, individuals and the business community seek arbitrage opportunities between government commitments and actual delivery. My own country, the United Kingdom, which has stumbled in recent years due to Brexit and other disasters (Boris Johnson notably) has actually done a sterling job in preparing the ground and executing smart climate policies. As Akshat Rathi writes in *Bloomberg Green*,[16] in 2008, over two-thirds of the people polled in the country said that the government should do more on climate (according to an IPSOS-Mori poll from that year). The same year the UK passed the Climate Change Act. Only five

[15]I draw on my article in Forbes, October 15, 2021 – China's Electricity Crisis – Don't Blame It on Renewables.
[16]Rathi writes the Net Zero column for Bloomberg Green, July 5, 2022.

members voted against the bill in Parliament, out of more than 600. "Since then the UK has had five prime ministers. It has experienced two financial crisis, Brexit, one pandemic, and is currently suffering the highest inflation in 40 years," says Rathi, "Yet each successive leader has only strengthened climate goals. The act's initial target was to cut emissions by 80% over 1990 levels by 2050. That has now been brought forward to 2035."

A strong legislative framework, broad public support, and a climate rule-book which guides how businesses should play their part is the UK's secret sauce in building momentum for change. The process is imperfect, as can be expected, with successive governments wrestling with energy shortages and a temptation to revert to business as usual, i.e., using fossil fuels, as Germany has been forced to do due to its overwhelming dependence on Russian natural gas imports. It must also be said that the political class in the UK is far more supportive compared with a section of the business community, where climate deniers still thrive.

In striking contrast to the UK, both America and Europe, where public support for governments to combat global warming are as high as the UK, fierce business lobbying (from the resources sector, no surprise here) and a lack of political will has held back progress. For leaders like Biden, who are genuinely committed to moving the needle, the compulsions of dealing with politics *du jour* have forced a rethink in energy policy. It is obvious that despite the rise of Tesla and electric vehicles, Americans remain addicted to traditional gasoline to fuel their gas guzzling vehicles. When gas prices rise, the federal government's perceived inaction is a favorite target of public wrath. The recently passed Inflation Reduction Act by Congress has reaffirmed America's commitment to address climate change but a periodic spike in gasoline prices will serve as a reminder that the country needs to do more.

There are some exceptions of course with the state of California, the world's sixth largest economy if 2021 gross state product of $3.4 trillion is stacked against other nations, has taken a progressive approach toward climate change. Even before the UK enshrined legally binding emission targets in 2008, California was already there by passing similar legislation two years earlier, requiring the state to cut greenhouse gas emissions to 1990 levels by

2020, which was achieved early by 2016. Besides its progressive strain of politics, why is California treating the climate crisis as an emergency? "... Californians have been suffering the effects of climate change for years," notes *The Economist*,[17] "Wildfires have incinerated towns and their smoke has dirtied the air. Drought has dried up water supplies. Extreme heat has baked cities and farms. And rising seas threaten coastal towns." California's climate distress, which it can manage because of its wealth and public support, mirrors the challenges faces by poor nations at the frontline of similar challenges, who of course have little resources to deploy.

So what are the building blocks for a smooth and just energy transition – so that we can graduate from current halting efforts at decarbonization to bolder attempts to green the global economy? The World Economic Forum, which brings together the great and not-so-great corporate participants, published an important report[18] spelling out what needs to be done. Some of the language is dense (even the Forum cannot escape corporate gobbledegook!) but the underlying points frame the issue well.

- First, countries have their "respective challenges" and needs in transitioning their energy systems to become more sustainable. The solution is in "continuously" transforming to respond to global challenges. Translation: all countries should embark on energy transition now but the speed of adjustment will vary.

- Second, the just transition toward sustainable energy will require huge amounts of financing. This challenge has been exacerbated by the pandemic. This is self-explanatory – the pandemic has left a gaping hole in public finances in many developing countries, just at a time of rising pressure to decarbonize.

- Third, a just energy transition will require "changes and shifts" in technologies, jobs, and other economic opportunities. New

---

[17]California wants to lead the world on climate policy – *The Economist*, April 23, 2022.
[18]Why justice must prevail as the world transitions to clean energy? – World Economic Forum, May 11, 2022.

skills, capacities, and expertise should be domestically developed to support the transformational processes. Sustainable energy can enable such a transformation but it must be made accessible and affordable.

The Forum report squarely places attention on people, a similar approach taken by the International Energy Agency (IEA), which established a global commission in 2021 to make recommendations on "people-centred clean energy transitions".[19] In a nutshell, the IEA report says that clean energy transitions will create jobs, enhance our quality of life, and ensure a cleaner, healthier environment. "A people-centred approach ensures the benefits and costs involved in the transformation of our energy system are distributed fairly and in a way that protects the most vulnerable in society. People-centered clean energy transition requires a focus on skills, decent jobs and worker protection, social and economic development, equity, social inclusion and fairness, and engaging people as active participants." At first glance, these appear to be motherhood statements, a laundry list of everything the world needs to in order to secure a just energy transition.

While I support the intent and objectives set out by the IEA and the Forum, I do notice a major gap – the role of business. Our carbon-industrial complex can only be scaled down with the active support of companies to reduce the carbon intensity of their operations. Time for a joke. Four fossil-fuel CEOs enter a bar. The bar-tender asks. "The usual?" One of them responds, "I will have mine with extra smog."

The motivations and machinations of big business should be central to any public policy conversation about climate change and social policy. The DNA of business leaders, as we will discuss in the next chapter, is inherently ill-designed to consider these issues. While there are certain segments of business which are trail-blazers in transport electrification, Tesla for example, there are hundreds of others who prefer business as usual as their operating mantra. How

[19]Recommendations of the Global Commission on People-Centred Clean Energy Transitions – published by the International Energy Agency, October 2021.

to motivate the business community with a set of carrots and incentives to decarbonize will be the defining challenge of our generation. It is too easy to maintain the status quo, even new ones. Steel and cement manufacturing, both critical to the modern economy, are labeled as "hard-to-abate" sectors because of the carbon intensity of their operations. Steel manufacturing is a $1 trillion plus industry globally with a massive carbon footprint – any effort to decarbonize the production process away from conventional blast furnace technologies will be a huge dividend for the planet. The fact that some start-ups in America are attempting to achieve this is encouraging.

When Amazon Web Services and several of its peers (Microsoft, Google) persuaded companies to take their data to the cloud, it launched a new, more efficient business model for companies to manage their information technology needs without the need to maintain costly in-house infrastructure. Few analysts paused for a moment and questioned the energy intensity of giant cloud server farms or data centers, which were overwhelmingly powered by conventional fossil fuels. The northern Virginia suburb of Loudon County is home to several of these data centers – large, impersonal, windowless structures – which process masses of corporate data without much human intervention in sight. At one level, the management of corporate data by outsourced providers is a business case study of how technology companies are taking over corporate data management. The efficiency gains, however, will not amount to much if the data centers are emitting carbon. Which is why AWS' commitment to powering its operations by 100% renewable energy by 2025 should be closely monitored.

Similarly, there is considerable hype about the merits of a circular economy and resource efficiency, keywords which business leaders like to throw around whenever they face difficult questions about the environmental intensity of their operations. The rationale for resource efficiency and a circular economy, which are often used interchangeably and generally mean the same thing, is sound and reasonable. Companies have to become much more efficient in the consumption of energy and materials in their production process, which over time will help in reducing their carbon footprint. The Environmental Protection Agency (EPA) in America has a precise definition[20] for the circular economy. "... refers to an economy that uses a systems-based approach and involves industrial processes and economic activities to maintain their highest value for as long as possible, and aims for the elimination of waste through the superior design of materials, products, and systems." These are commendable objectives but some head-scratching is inevitable. Investors and other stakeholders generally want business to be mindful in managing material resources. A car manufacturer wants to produce to full capacity by wisely using inputs such as steel and ensure that any waste at the end of the process is recycled. My point is that this should be given across the corporate sector and not positioned as an amazing new solution to reduce emissions and warming of the planet.

This brings me to cryptocurrencies. When the eponymous Satoshi Nakamoto unleashed the Bitcoin and the blockchain on an unsuspecting world in 2008, it was regarded as a bold step forward in decentralizing the global economy. It took some time for policymakers in China, the first hub for Bitcoin mining, to figure out that miners were draining enormous energy resources to generate a cryptocurrency of questionable value. This comment will no doubt enrage crypto enthusiasts but Bitcoin and its bandwagon of digital tokens and currencies are simply not viable until the energy intensity issue has been resolved. There are much broader questions about the role of such coins and tokens in modern finance which are the beyond the scope of this book. The Columbia Climate School[21] estimates that Bitcoin currently consumes 150 terawatt[22] hours of electricity annually – more than the entire country of Argentina, population 45 million. "Producing that energy emits some 65 megatons of carbon dioxide into the atmosphere annually – comparable to the emissions of

---

[20]What is a circular economy? United States EPA, National Recycling Strategy, November 29, 2021.
[21]Cryptocurrency's dirty secret: Energy Consumption – Columbia Climate School, May 4, 2022.
[22]A terawatt is a unit of power equivalent to one trillion watts. In simple terms, 1 terawatt can power 10 billion, 100 watt bulbs at the same time.

Greece – making crypto a significant contributor to global air pollution and climate change."

The world seems to be sleep-walking toward a carbon-heavy future by taking expensive detours into the circular economy, energy-guzzling data centers, and cryptocurrencies. This is where corporate leadership can make a difference. Do business leaders have what it takes to integrate nonfinancial metrics like the environmental and social impact into their strategy and operations? We turn to this in our next chapter.

4

THE PROPHET MOTIVE

Why Short-Termism in Business and the Profit Motive Collides With Nonfinancial and Longer Term Environmental and Social Challenges.

When the wheels of modern capitalism traverse through the narrow streets of the square mile that is the City of London or New York's Wall Street, there is a particular group of actors who are watching its every move. Sitting on the side-lines, as they are often accused of, this group has the power to make and unmake corporate titans and the listed companies they represent. They are the ultimate bean-counters as they dissect corporate strategies and break down a company's earnings potential, quarter over quarter, and disseminate this insight to anxious investors and the public at large. When French *la nouvelle vague* director Jean-Luc Godard once proclaimed that "cinema is truth, at 24 frames per second," these capitalist avatars are likely to say, "our financial spreadsheets are corporate truth, every ninety days over ninety days."

Behold the power of the analyst who makes a living looking under the hood of listed companies, large and small. There are analysts and analysts of course. The tribe we are focusing on are known as equity analysts. They have counterparts in bond markets and the broader macroeconomic space, who wield equal power and influence to shape their respective areas of influence. However, for the purposes of the book our area of focus is on the inscrutable equity analyst, who come rain or shine offers daily commentary on a company's current and future performance and sticks a convenient label against the stock – sell, buy, or hold.

I have been both a journalist and a corporate insider and watched the grip which analysts and their reports have on the fate of the company and the stability of the C-suite. Corporate CEOs and analysts have a love-hate relationship – the analysts genuinely love the companies they cover and the CEOs, with some exceptions, hate them with a passion. In the eyes of the corporate master of the universe, who typically presides over a complex international enterprise with hundreds of thousands of staff in multiple geographies, the analyst is like a pesky fly buzzing around the corporate suite dodging every attempt to be swatted. From the perspective of the corporate CEO, how could an analyst poring over spreadsheets possibly know more about the company than he or she is leading? When a negative analyst's report lands on the desk of a company's investor relations team, a valiant attempt to made to provide a gloss over the brutal content. Switching metaphors, the analysts regard themselves as a group of canaries in the coal mine, providing early warning to investors about toxic corporate performance and behaviors.

This does not happen all of the time as the Wirecard saga in Germany amply demonstrated. Listed on the Deutsche Borse in Germany (and since delisted), Wirecard is a cautionary tale of investor and analyst enthusiasm about a company's business model (in payments and fin-tech) and relentless efforts by management to sell a fabricated narrative to mislead on a massive scale. Wirecard had a market capitalization of $27 billion in 2018 and the German company was feted for its approach in facilitating payments in difficult emerging markets. It was up to intrepid investigative reporters of the *Financial Times* to dig deep into the company's murky finances to discover that Wirecard was a financial house of cards – the 1.9 billion euros in cash listed on its balance sheet did not exist, although validated by auditing firm EY. My point here is that if the analyst community gets things fundamentally wrong in its core business of financial forensics, there is a greater possibility of errors in judgment and fact when it comes to analyzing complex ESG issues like carbon emissions or diversity and inclusion data.

An additional problem is the adulation (by media and analysts) of superstar CEOs – a label which originated with the American business media's adulation of the late Jack Welch, CEO of storied engineering firm GE which has stumbled in recent years with strong evidence to show that many of the problems originated during Welch's tenure as highlighted in an earlier chapter. A focus on personalities, as happened in the Wirecard saga, detracts from the real business of analyzing a company's performance across financial and non-financial yardsticks. The current group of superstar CEOs in America and Europe, as worshipped by media and analysts alike, includes the likes of Elon Musk (Tesla), Jamie Dimon (JP Morgan), and Bernard Arnault (luxury goods conglomerate LVMH). Without taking away the important role that leadership plays in corporate performance, our obsession with personalities gets in the way of understanding the true nature and intent of a corporation.

There is also the group of superstar analysts to contend with, the most prominent of them from a previous era on Wall Street being Abby Joseph Cohen, the high priestess of market gurus whose every proclamation moved the market. Here is a sampler[1] from 2000. "Market guru (Abby Joseph) Cohen yesterday advised her Goldman Sachs & Co. clients to invest less in stocks and hold more cash, and to reduce their technology holdings. Her remarks, which represented a modest backing off from her previous bullish stance, were broadcast to the public before the markets opened and had an immediate impact, sending stock prices lower." At one stage in the early 2000s, Cohen was regarded by financial markets to be as influential, if not more, as Alan Greenspan, the Delphic Chairman of the Federal Reserve whose own reputation has been damaged since the global financial crisis.

The inescapable conclusion that I draw is that the toxic short-term focus on corporate and economic performance has had far reaching implications on the world we live in. The symbiotic relationship between corporate CEOs, analysts, and media has reinforced short-term behaviors in financial markets, with a rigid focus on the here and now and with the profit motive at all costs. In

---

[1]Abby Joseph Cohen's Words Move Markets – *The Washington Post*, March 29, 2000.

management meetings and business reviews, CEOs often ask "can we make the quarter," worrying that weak performance in a specific business could torpedo carefully choreographed quarterly forecasts, which are already built into future earnings and the current share price of the company. Although the correlation does not work perfectly, weak performance should typically translate into lower remuneration and benefits for the C-suite. Issuing a negative profit warning, the worse cast scenario for many CEOs, also shows them up to be weak and inefficient managers. If one had to make a visual representation of a CEO attempting to meet quarterly forecasts, it would be that of the Stairmaster at your local gym where you must keep on climbing to stay on top of a performance target. Above all, the short-termism which pervades corporate America and Europe (the latter to a far lesser extent) conflicts and contradicts with the business community's desire to be a good corporate citizen – which requires attention on medium and long-term goals of protecting the planet and investing in people.

Unsurprisingly, the list of corporate titans who focus on long-term performance metrics is a small list indeed. Billionaire Warren Buffet, who has long railed against the obsession with quarterly performance, is a rare example of someone who has bucked the trend. Indeed, if Buffett were starting out today as a financial adviser attempting to push his investment philosophy, he would probably be fired notes UBS analyst Michael Crook.[2] "The high long-term returns achieved by Berkshire Hathaway required patience through extended underperformance. My conclusion: since most investors would fire Warren Buffett, they are also probably too quick to sell something out of a portfolio when it hasn't worked over 1–5 years."

Over this time horizon, Buffett's conglomerate has outperformed in the past and generated returns of over 350% to investors. I make this point not because Berkshire Hathaway is the poster child for long-range ESG thinking in business (to be clear, it is not) but to illustrate how rare it is to think in years rather than quarters on Wall Street. In 2015, I was part of a small group put together by consulting

[2]Fire Warren Buffett? Investors Obsessed with Quarterly Performance Probably Would – *CNBC*, March 12, 2019.

firm McKinsey on a project, ambitiously titled "Focusing Capital on the Long-Term[3] (or FCLT for short)." The project was unusual[4] in the sense that it was sponsored by a global consulting firm whose clients are obsessed with short-term performance and indeed my co-collaborators were representatives of many of these entities.

The premise of the FCLT project was that improving the flow of information and ideas between investors and corporates on long-term issues could help counteract the short-term bias inherent in business decisions. The focus on short-term actions and communications, we noted, seem counterproductive, considering that when experts deconstruct the value expectations embedded in share prices, 70%–90% of a company's value is related to cash flows expected three or more years out. In plain English, this means that the implied value of a company's current share price factors in money which the company is likely to generate in the next few years. Nevertheless, corporate short-termism rules and leads to what we described as "value destroying behaviors." "One survey found that 55% of CFOs, would avoid undertaking an NPV (net present value)-positive investment if it meant falling short of the quarter's consensus earnings per share. And 78% of executives said they would take actions to improve quarterly earnings at the expense of long-term value creation. Companies that expressly seek to manage short-term earnings to narrowly beat consensus also under-perform peers after two years."

There is a lot to unpack here so it is useful to consider the full impact of what the survey findings cited above means in terms of senior management behaviors. First, most Chief Financial Officers of companies, a position which is typically No. 2 or 3 in the C-suite hierarchy, would avoid making a positive longer-term investment today if it meant that it translates into a short-term hit on quarterly earnings. An even bigger segment of corporate executives said that quarterly earnings targets matter most, long-term value creation be damned. The point to emphasize is that the FCLT project was focused squarely on how to create long-term value for investors on

---

[3]Straight Talk for the long term – An in-depth look at improving the investor-corporate dialogue – report published March 2015.
[4]Also unusual for the pre-pandemic era was that the entire project discussions were conducted online.

a set of financial rather than the popular ESG metrics which are all the rage today. If we had to go back in time to 2015, the year when the Paris Climate accord was negotiated, it is fair to state that while long-term environmental and social considerations were generating some corporate attention at the time, they were mainly regarded as a reputational challenge for companies to overcome. The focus was on improving the "narrative" and inoculating companies from reputation risk by enthusiastically championing globally negotiated deals like the Paris accord and the United Nations Sustainable Development Goals, which came into effect the same year. Many companies invested in expensive PR and advertising campaigns supporting the SDGs, or global goals for short, and it very likely that C-suite executives of these firms were the ones responding to survey questions highlighted above.

We will discuss in detail later how companies and CEOs should embrace and integrate what I describe as societal thinking into their strategy and operations. Returning to the FCLT, our group made three simple recommendations to foster long-term thinking of business in the dialogue between corporates and investors, with analysts playing a critical role as knowledge intermediaries in this process. The first recommendation was self-explanatory – build a compelling long-term strategy and communicate it to investors. I quote, "Management must credibly explain to investors how its strategy creates long-term value and strengthens competitive advantage. Communications from management to investors regarding strategy should include enough evidence to substantiate the company's position and direction."

This is easier said than done as I have discovered in my corporate experience and witness to many a grand "strategy day," targeting a gaggle of investors and analysts. Companies tend to refresh their strategy for one of three reasons – the current strategy is clearly not working, a new CEO has arrived and does not want to have anything to do with the previous management team and their strategy, or short-sellers and activist investors are knocking on the company's doors and an urgent strategy refresh is needed. The time horizon of a typical strategy deck, as it is known, is three years with the CEO taking investors and analysts on a narrative journey on how the strategic goals will be accomplished. The metrics are all financial – growth in top line, cost base, and bottom line, and return on equity are what the markets want to learn from nonfinancial companies and all the above plus the cost of capital and pace of loan impairments if you happen to be a bank. The refreshed strategy is usually based on what the CEO would regard as foundational truths about the company – its unique business proposition, market leadership, intellectual property, and competitive pressures which could undermine all the three. Although the CEO is attempting to "sell" a longer-term story to markets, all that the investment community wants to hear is if the company is going to be healthy enough to generate short-term returns and justify their continued attention and resources. My takeaway is that simply focusing attention on the long term, which was the objective of our project, is not enough.

Our second recommendation – measure long-term value creation and performance relative to a set of long-term metrics specific to the company's long-term strategy – goes to the heart of the problem. "A well-articulated strategy must include metrics that allow companies and investors to track progress against strategic objectives and assess the company's ability to deliver value over an extended time horizon," the report said, "Developing and integrating such metrics into company and investor decision-making and compensation structures is essential in order to migrate the investor-corporate dialogue toward a more balanced discussion about a company's short-and-long-term prospects." A critical delivery for this will be in the development of sector-specific and company-specific metrics which monitor and disclose performance over a longer period. ESG fits neatly into this template because the environmental and social impact of a business cannot be boiled down to a set of short-term disclosures. What would be meaningful disclosure for investors would be a three-or-five-year trend-line of a company's carbon emissions, rather than quarter-over-quarter developments.

There are sharp divergences in attitudes toward long-term planning between Anglo-American and continental European corporate structures. A typical Anglo-American response to long-term corporate planning, as I have learned, is one of the following two. First, Keynes is inevitably invoked and his quote "in the long-run we are all dead" offered as a reason why the utility of long-term planning is questionable.

Second, long-term planning is compared with Soviet central planning and regarded as a failed "socialist" effort. I have heard arguments to the effect that modern capitalism and capital markets, developed and perfected in the UK and America, were inherently designed for price discovery based on short-term performance. Reconfiguring this proposition will destroy the very nature of capitalism, so the argument goes. The evidence in favor of this does not stack up because even that most capitalist of creatures, the banker and investor, still wants to know how a particular company is likely to perform financially over the medium-term.

Over in Europe, the ethos is at sharp variance from the Anglo-Saxon model with the heavy hand of European Union (and national government) intervention in almost every aspect of a corporation's existence. It was the European Union rather than America's FTC which placed a regulatory floor against monopolistic practices of America's Big Tech firms and in proposing pioneering but unimplementable ideas in curbing cross-border emissions through a carbon adjustment tax. The European approach is derided as "socialist" by their Anglo-American counterparts, who point out that this is why Europe has lagged in building vibrant capital markets (the continent remains overwhelmingly dependent on bank lending, as noted earlier) and in encouraging the growth of entrepreneurship, Silicon Valley style.

Our third recommendation was on the nature and objectives of the investor class. "A well-developed strategy, supported by the right set of quantitative and qualitative metrics, can steer a business toward successful execution and value creation. By transparently reporting progress to investors in a way that fosters a long-term dialogue, companies can potentially reduce the volatility of their stock price along with their cost of capital," the report said. The hurdle here being the nature of the relationship between investors and companies, which has traditionally been positioned on short-term performance. "Fostering long-term dialogue is not solely the responsibility of companies. Long-term investors also have a substantial role to play in proactively engaging management and where appropriate, directors." Although long-term investors – asset managers like (BlackRock being a shining example) and pension funds have always positioned their investment approaches toward the long-term, I have observed that their time-horizon for performance is typically positioned on short-term expectations. On one level, this is understandable given that asset managers and pension funds are custodians of someone else's money and cannot blindly wait a few years for a company to raise its game. In the pre-ESG era, the typical conversation between a CEO/Chair of a major international bank and a long-term investor (LTI) proceeded along these lines:

CEO/Chair:	We have had a bad few quarters but believe that the worst is now behind us.
LTI:	Your competitors are performing better than you in the same geography.
CEO/Chair:	The next quarter results will show that we are catching up and I am confident that we will out-perform peers by the end of the year.
LTI:	Your EBITDA[5] forecasts seem stretched.
CEO/Chair:	We believe it is reasonable and achievable.

Now, I must tip my hat to the LTIs, who since the FCLT report was published in 2015 have dramatically changed their approach and attitudes toward corporate performance. A typical investor-corporate dialogue in circa 2022 between the same CEO and a long-term investor is likely to proceed on the following lines:

CEO/Chair:	This year is looking really good. EBITDA is up double digits and if all things go well, we will also consider a share buyback.
LTI:	Good but we worry about your continued exposure to fossil fuels. What is your climate change strategy?
CEO/Chair (nervously sipping water):	We are about to declare a net zero target and will be carbon free by 2050 like our peers.
LTI:	We will all be dead by then (laughter). But we want to see tangible progress in the next three years. What is your plan?

---

[5]For the uninitiated, EBITDA – earnings before interest, taxes, depreciation, and amortization – is a short-term indicator of the overall profitability of a company. If I ever opened a pub in the City, this would be the name!

| CEO/Chair: | We have recruited a head of sustainability and will be discussing our strategy later in the year. |
| LTI: | We see climate change as the highest priority for companies we invest in and would like you to report back soon when the plan is finalized. |

Company executives reading this hypothetical conversation are likely to object because I have reduced the CEO/Chair in the conversation to be ill-informed about ESG issues and ready to delegate climate change to the newly arriving head of sustainability. While I may have taken some (artistic) liberties, I acknowledge it may well be true that American and European C-suites are filled with progressive business leaders who want to do the right thing. The problem is that this group is very small, as Paul Polman would attest, and a majority of the corporate elite deploy rhetoric and high purpose on sustainability without backing this up with concrete long-term ESG metrics.

There are some exceptions and here is a good example from the website of global mining giant Rio Tinto, which has been through a damaging operational event. "We have had some difficult conversations, both within our business and with stakeholders, about our actions, performance, and culture. This feedback has helped shape a new direction for our leadership team, and our business as a whole." If you are unfamiliar with Rio Tinto, you are right to wonder what the difficult conversations cited in the website may possibly refer to. Well, let's discover the 46,000-year-old Juukan Gorge in Western Australia, which is rich in the country's Aboriginal heritage. The problem (and opportunity) for Rio Tinto was that also nestled in the area under the gorge were sizable iron ore deposits which it intended to extract and exploit for commercial gain.

Exhibit A in this case is the gorge itself, which *The Guardian*[6] described as "one of the only sites on the Pilbara to show continued human occupation through the last ice age, and archeological records,

[6]Rio Tinto blew up Jukaan Gorge rock shelters to "access higher volumes of high-grade iron ore", *The Guardian*, August 4, 2020, and an earlier report on the blowing up of the gorge itself.

including bone pits that cataloged changing fauna, dated back 46,000 years." As early as 1972, an Australian minister had declared that the "preservation of sites and objects of Aboriginal origin is now recognised throughout Australia as an important aspect of providing Aboriginal citizens with the social environment that they need when to still retain partly or wholly their traditional beliefs." Anyone familiar with Australia's cruel heritage in destroying Aboriginal society and their culture will recognize that destroying a 46,000-year-old site held sacred by the country's original population is not the way to protect their rights.

Exhibit B was Rio Tinto's claims over the commercial value of the site. A report from July 2011[7] notes that Brockman 4, which includes the Jukaan gorge, comprises "600 million tonnes of ore" over a sprawling area covering 80,000 square miles. At an average iron ore price of approximately $130 per ton, the overall deposit at the site is valued at a phenomenal $78 billion, yes $78 billion. With these long-term economics in mind, what does Rio Tinto do? The answer came in May 2020, when the world was pre-occupied with the pandemic, Rio Tinto proceeded with commercial exploitation (after receiving approval from the western Australian provincial authorities) by blowing up the gorge and the 46,000-year-old heritage along with it. For the technically minded on how the company blew up the gorge, the company disclosed that it had drilled 382 blast holes and loaded them up with explosives, even though the local Aboriginal community learned of the plan and attempted to stop it.

To the world's credit and despite the pandemic, there was global outrage over the destruction of Juukan gorge, which many compared with the Taliban's blowing up of the much more recent Bamiyan Buddhas in 2001, which date back to the sixth century. "Rio Tinto has unreservedly apologised to the Puutu Kunti Kurrama and Pinkura people (PKKP)[8] and we reaffirm that apology now," the company's official submission after the destruction reads, "For the benefit of current and future generations of Australians, we are determined to learn the lessons to ensure that the destruction of heritage sites of

---

[7]Rio Tinto Brockman 4 Iron Ore Mine, Pilbara – Mining Technology, July 27, 2011.
[8]The PKKP are the aboriginal community native to the resource rich Pilbara region in Western Australia.

exceptional archeological and cultural significance, such as the Jukaan rock shelters, never occurs again." The destruction of Juukan cost Rio Tinto CEO Jean-Sebastien Jacques his job, which is small comfort for the PKKP community's profound sense of loss over their heritage. Rio Tinto's behavior in the run-up to the destruction of the gorge is sadly all too common in the fossil fuels, mining, and forestry industries. There is a rush to judgment and unseemly haste to act when it comes to serving the profit motive and all other considerations are set aside. Much of this, in my view, has to do with "corporate culture" and the distorted incentive structure within large corporations. Corporate culture first. The modern corporation is a lot like Japan in terms of homogeneity. While Japan takes pride in the fact that over 95% of the country's population are comprised of Japanese ethnicity,[9] the modern corporation is composed exclusively of people who belong to one or two of the following categories of professionals – finance, legal, taxation, risk, HR staff, and those with specific domain expertise depending on the primary business of the organization – geologists in the case of Rio Tinto, the technologists who populate Silicon Valley, and bankers on Wall Street and in the City. What brings this seemingly disparate group together into a homogenous cluster is worship of business and the bottom-line. This is not a value judgment but a fact. Homogenous or majoritarian societies like Japan or Germany may flourish, but it becomes a significant barrier when everyone thinks and acts like one in a modern corporation. Here is a snapshot of the educational backgrounds of CEOs of the top five international banks in America:

Jamie Dimon (JP Morgan) – Harvard University (MBA)

Brian Moynihan (Bank of America) – University of Notre Dame (law)

David Solomon (Goldman Sachs) – Hamilton College[10] (BA)

James Gorman (Morgan Stanley) – Columbia University (MBA)

Jane Fraser (Citibank) – Harvard University (MBA).

---

[9]This claim about Japanese ethnic homogeneity has been contested by many scholars, read, for example "How homogenous is Japan" by Noah Smith, December 10, 2020.
[10]Solomon graduated in political science and worked his way up the ladder at Goldman Sachs. Unlike most CEOs, he is also a well-known DJ, specializing in electronic dance music.

The corporate purists are likely to push-back at my assertion of educational homogeneity amongst America's top banking CEOs. They have a point. You have to be business-trained and have the right background to aspire to work or run one of America's top corporations. However, there are societal costs to this homogeneity as we have discovered with Wall Street banks headlong plunge into toxic mortgage-backed securities (MBS) in the run-up to the 2008 global financial crisis. The system does have checks and balances, through corporate governance rules and regulations supervised by the SEC and similar agencies in Europe. But inside the corporation, it was arguably very difficult in the pre-2008 period for someone to take a contrarian view on MBS and their potential to blow up the balance sheets of the biggest banks, imposing huge costs on society in the process. The monoculture of the modern corporation, as I have learned in my own stint in the private sector, does not reward contrarian thinking and anyone who dares to challenge the status quo is likely to face a turbulent and brief career. These risks are compounded when it comes to ESG – where C-suites are singularly ill-equipped to understand and manage the "tragedy of the horizon," as former Bank of England Governor Mark Carney described in his landmark speech in 2015 launching the central bank's focus on climate change. "Our societies face a series of profound environmental and social challenges," the Governor said,[11] "The combination of the weight of scientific evidence and the dynamics of the financial system suggests that, in the fullness of time, climate change will threaten financial resilience and longer-term prosperity." He ended his speech by saying that by "managing what gets measured, we can break the Tragedy of the Horizon."

Managing what gets measured, in Carney's memorable words, is ESG's biggest operational challenge. The typical CEO and his/her management cohort, schooled in spreadsheets and financial targets, find it very difficult to grasp the scientific evidence of accelerating climate change and the societal impact of their business. The "make the quarter" business philosophy is in conflict with the company's ability to take a longer-term view, which will require painful

---

[11]Breaking the tragedy of the horizon – climate change and financial stability – speech by Mark Carney, September 29, 2015.

decisions like withdrawing from energy-intensive businesses and to ask hard questions about abuses in the supply chain. All these decisions come with financial strings attached and a new business mindset, let's call it the prophet motive, where companies' desire to make a positive impact on society, is balanced with the profit motive. This will require training staff at all levels within the organization and the MBA factories of the world also have a role in training the business leaders of tomorrow. Although the MBA "brand" has somewhat lost its sheen in recent years, many leading business schools have reconfigured their offering to include ESG and Sustainability modules. "A decade ago, the hottest MBA courses typically covered topics such as game theory, valuing securities, and negotiating mergers," *The New York Times*[12] reported, "Today, some of the most popular classes are about climate finance, impact investing, and social entrepreneurship." While this is an encouraging trend, the business courses on offer is unlikely to change behaviors of one segment of the business community – Silicon Valley founders, where the mythology is to drop out of college and plunge headlong into starting a successful tech venture.

In the near-term, corporations are attempting to mitigate the lack of formal ESG training by taking a duct tape approach to these problems – restructuring the sustainability function, for example, and creating a Chief Sustainability Officer (CSO) role as a way of being visibly taking action on curbing emissions or in diversity. At the same time, the CSO in a bank is also responsible for drumming up business for sustainable finance, creating a clear conflict of interest in governance. Anxious to "make the quarter", there is every possibility that the CSO would ride rough-shod over the environmental and social risk function to validate deals even if they don't strictly comply on ESG grounds.

Having served as the head of sustainability myself, I will cheerfully admit that while I had responsibility over nonbusiness sustainability functions in the organization, I could not move the needle much on my own. A decision to withdraw from fossil fuels,

----

[12]Business Schools Respond to a Flood of interest in ESG – DealBook Newsletter, *The New York Times*, November 13, 2021.

for example, is intimately tied up with near-term financial impact, which only the CEO can take by bringing the top team along. In that sense, I see the CEO serving de facto as the Chief Sustainability Officer of the corporation, ensuring that ESG and sustainability considerations are factored in for every major corporate decision.

This approach will work only if the compensation and incentive structure of top management is heavily skewed in favor of long-term performance and transparent ESG metrics. No surprise that this is not the norm now but it is increasingly one. Global consulting firm PWC[13] notes that in the UK alone, around 45% of companies listed on the top level FTSE100 now have an ESG measure in executive pay and 78% of board members and senior executives agree that strong ESG performance contributes to organizational value and/or financial performance. "Increasing ESG metrics in executive pay packages is a tangible way to close the say-do gap for a skeptical audience, but it is not without its challenges," PWC analysts say, "There's a risk of hitting the target but missing the point. An example might be a bank that focuses on reducing its own carbon footprint when the biggest effect it could have on reducing its emissions is through changing its approach to financing companies which emit carbon." As we will discuss in the next chapter, companies are finding it easier to manage their own emissions (Scope 1 and 2) rather than go through the trouble of calculating the emissions of their clients and suppliers (Scope 3).

There are also risks that linking pay with ESG metrics, which might tempt CEOs to go on over-drive in articulating the company's social purpose and in building what I would describe as "light," easy to achieve KPIs (which partially explains C-suites obsession with planting trees, for example). "There's often an idea that ESG targets in pay can be used to direct CEOs to undertake activities that benefit society, which they wouldn't undertake without the incentive," the PWC report notes, "This misunderstands how Board governance works. Pay follows strategy; it doesn't drive strategy. But once ESG factors are integrated into the strategy, linking them to pay can be a natural next step, particularly as a tool for mobilizing the organisation behind a new

---

[13]Linking executive pay to ESG goals – PWC, June 29, 2021.

set of priorities." There must be costs to compensation if the CEO and the team achieve financial metrics during the year but fail on any of the ESG metrics. A spectacular example is Rio Tinto and the exit of its CEO after the destruction of the Jukaan gorge. Any ESG-linked compensation structure should be linked with specific long-term goals, which we will turn to in the next three chapters.

5

THE 'E' OF 'ESG'

EMISSION OMISSIONS

As the World Races to Achieve Net Zero Emissions, the Business Community Has to Play a Decisive Role. Are CEOs Ready?

Everyone in business wants to be a hero (or heroine) in netting out carbon emissions.

Let's bring back the CEO of the major international bank whom we encountered in the previous chapter, the one who was nervously sipping water when a long-term investor quizzed him about the bank's climate strategy and net zero plan. I must add a disclaimer,

Hollywood movie style: the CEO I am portraying is entirely fictional and no identification with actual CEOs in banking or otherwise is intended or should be inferred. Let's move ahead on this basis. The prized head of sustainability has arrived and the CEO, bracing from the conversation with one of his most important shareholders, wants to act and wants to be seen acting in the interests of society. He does what CEOs do best when faced with a tough management decision – he convenes a leadership retreat, or offsite as it is popularly referred to. This is what CEOs usually do at the end or beginning of the financial year to motivate and energize their top teams, announce major investment decisions, and to make the tough call on reducing costs. I have attended a fair number of these leadership retreats in my time and they all have a familiar ring to them. During the day, various members of the leadership team make elaborate presentations to impress their peers. The Chief Financial Officer provides an optimistic (or pessimistic) assessment of the company's financial position, and a prominent local luminary is wheeled in (usually over dinner) to pontificate about pressing global issues of the day. At night, the action moves to the bar as bottles and bottles of champagne and fine wines are uncorked and the leadership team parties well into the night. In the parlance of the management coaching industry, this is known as team bonding.

The problem is that most CEOs and their leadership teams are singularly ill-equipped to deal with environmental issues or indeed loftier issues like the role of their business in saving the planet. Let's take our own CEO as an illustrative example. He has risen up the ranks in investment banking, working in a succession of top roles all over the world. In the rarefied circles which he travels in, he is known as a "rainmaker," the investment banker with a consistent track record in landing some of the biggest deals and the juiciest fees. He is comfortable navigating deal term-sheets and chewing his peers and juniors about intricate details of a financial transaction. Take him away from this comfort zone and the CEO begins to waffle when asked about the bank's ESG proposition.

More recently, our CEO has been forced to devote more time to ESG issues because an international NGO has been running a global campaign against the bank. The NGO has raised attention that the bank under his leadership happens to be the single biggest financiers of fossil fuels and forestry, therefore playing a significant role in warming the planet and destroying livelihoods of those on the frontline of climate distress. NGO protestors even showed up outside bank headquarters to press their case and outside the CEOs house one early morning when he was enjoying his breakfast, to the horror of family and neighbors in his posh central London neighborhood. The CEOs children, who are millennials and socially progressive, are beginning to fret about negative comments made by friends about their Dad's role and are pressuring him to do something positive about climate change. This combined with investor pressure has motivated the CEO to recruit a head of sustainability from a rival bank and he assumes that this will buy him some time and the "environmental problem," as he describes it, will either be addressed to the full satisfaction of external stakeholders or will simply fade away in importance over time.

He is wrong on the latter as the leadership retreat makes clear. The head of sustainability, a former policymaker and sustainability expert of repute, is no wall-flower and calmly presents the sober case that the Bank has to urgently adjust its business model. She points out that the international NGO is absolutely right in asserting that their bank is right up there in the global league table of financial institutions supporting fossil fuel and forestry industries. Indeed, lending into these sectors, by the bank's own disclosures, accounted for a hefty 40% of revenue and over two-thirds of profits in the latest financial year. The direct environmental impact of such lending, she estimates, accounted for 60 million tons of the bank's annual Scope 3 emissions. The bank had disclosed intentions of achieving a net zero target of 2050 under investor pressure, she notes, but very little work had actually been done in implementing the plan. Her immediate mandate, she pointedly notes, was to get the bank "over the line" on its regulatory requirements and to ensure that climate and ESG elements are integrated into business strategy, with a defined pathway away from fossil fuels and forestry lending.

The room erupts in anger and confusion. Until the head of sustainability made her presentation, bankers in the room were coasting along, nursing a hangover from the previous night's excesses and poking fun at colleagues. This was a jovial, collegial group which had just been jolted into reality. They know that pulling away from fossil fuels and forestry, with no viable alternative business in sight, would destroy the bank's fortunes and their bonuses. Who exactly was this interloper on the stage bossing them around, the new head of sustainability who has barely been around a few weeks to tell them that their cushy business model had to be dismantled.

Watching the furore from the leadership team with alarm, the CEO intervenes and takes to the stage. He does what he should have done at the start of the retreat – not glossed over the bank's external challenges with long-term investors and NGOs over the bank's environmental footprint. This is the time for candid truth-telling and he should not have set up what looks like an ambush of the new head of sustainability, dooming her job prospects even before she had a chance of proving her mettle. The CEO calms the leadership mob and starts behaving like the Chief Sustainability Officer he should be. He recounts his own uncomfortable conversations with long-term investors and family over the bank's huge emissions footprint and asserts that if the bank did not change course, it would lose the support of a significant section of the investor community. The regulators were also snapping at the bank's heels, with new disclosure requirements under the Task-force for Climate Financial Disclosures (TCFD for short) coming into effect by 2025.

Using the best phraseology from the strategy day, the CEO pledges to refresh the business model, reenergize leadership team and staff, and reinforce the central message that the bank was a positive force for the planet. Even the most hardened banker in the audience, whose personal finances have been replenished over the years from fossil fuel clients, is moved by the CEO's intervention and there is loud applause. Using the favorable momentum to his advantage, the CEO goes on offsite mode and asks his head of sustainability to divide up the room into two groups. The first group, Group A, to discuss and determine how the bank should curb its own emissions (Scope 1 and 2), a second group, Group B, which includes the CEO to figure out the pathways and costs of exiting fossil fuels and forestry, which will lead to a sharp reduction in Scope 3 emissions, and to establish new source of businesses to replace the loss in revenue and profits from fossil fuel and forestry financing. Flip chart easels, marker pens, and Post-it notes are wheeled in for the two groups to come up with a plan.

It is useful to digress from the proceedings of the retreat, which we shall return to shortly, to focus on the regulatory pressure on banks, asset managers, and insurers to dramatically reduce emissions. TCFD, as highlighted earlier, was the brainchild of former Bank of England Governor Mark Carney, who put together a global group of financial worthies in 2014 to come up with a cohesive plan to strengthen greater disclosure of the financial sector to its exposure to fossil fuels and other climate-destroying activities. The proposition being that greater financial disclosure will help long-term investors make informed decisions about which climate friendly companies to support and put their trillions of dollars capital in and more crucially which ones to withdraw from. TCFD is designed to address the biggest nightmare of bankers and long-term investors which arise from stranded assets, i.e., assets as defined by the Lloyds of London[1] that have suffered from "unanticipated or premature" write-downs, devaluations, or conversion into liabilities. "Changes to the physical environment driven by climate change and society's response to these changes, could potentially strand entire regions and global industries within a short time-frame, leading to the direct and indirect impacts on investment strategies and liabilities." For example, if a bank is overexposed to the coal mining and coal-fired power generation sectors and regulatory and societal pressures forces the country to switch to renewable power sources, there is considerable risk that the long-term financing provided by the bank to projects and clients will become stranded – since the underlying asset no longer generates economic value and will potentially lead to a write-off. Bankers and investors hate loan write-offs since it diminishes capital and earning potential, reducing profits, return on equity, and bonuses of the CEO and the top team.

To return to our CEO and his leadership retreat, this is the case he is calmly building up in Group B, that changing the bank's business model was not only mandated by society – regulators,

---

[1]Stranded assets – the transition to a low carbon economy – Lloyd's of London, February 23, 2017.

investors, and the public at large – but was also central to the institution's very existence. There is nervous energy in Group B, as the message from the CEO sinks in and the bankers realize that this is no ordinary retreat question which they can easily forget about during this evening's cocktail hour. The survival instinct is strong amongst bankers and they turn to the task at hand with relish. Sensing the momentum, the CEO stands next to the flip chart, and canvasses views from the table on three questions he has written down?

Is there a viable way of sustaining lending into fossil fuels and improving client behaviors?

What is the role of carbon capture, utilization, and storage, and carbon trading markets to mitigate the damage from continued emissions by the fossil fuels sector?

What would a plan to double down on sustainable finance look like? How soon can the bank replace the loss from financing fossil fuels?

Let's take each of these questions in turn, as the bankers engage in deep conversation with colleagues and place Post-It notes with suggestions on the flip chart. The first question on improving client behaviors in the fossil fuel industry is a loaded one. A simple answer, if one reads all of the commentary emanating from NGOs and climate experts, is that there should be an immediate, urgent halt to all fossil fuel production all over the world. This is clearly unrealistic since much of the developing world, as we discussed in a previous chapter, is heavily dependent on fossil fuels (coal in particular) to generate energy and power economic growth. A just energy transition will require some forbearance from developed countries in supporting the economic growth and opportunity aspirations of the developing world, by sharply reducing their own dependence on fossil fuels and providing "climate space" to poorer nations to still use fossil fuels. This is of course an incredibly contentious political issue and outside the scope of the work out-lined by the CEO for his leadership team. He simply wants to know if there are ways the bank could use its financial leverage to persuade and influence fossil fuel clients to pollute less and to speed up their transition into renewables, which many of the world's oil majors are already attempting to do. By achieving this, he argues, the bank will be on target to achieve net zero well before 2050 and assure investors that the institution is decarbonizing its business model.

There are sharp divisions on the table, as can be expected. One segment on the table, let's call them *The Protectors* regard themselves as self-appointed guardians of the bank. Arrayed against them on the table are a group of relative newcomers, much more exposed to the difficult external environment which expects radical change from business and away from fossil fuels. Let's call them *The Pragmatists*, who will advocate for a dramatic pivot to sustainable finance.

The Protectors first. Many of them had spent all of their working lives in this single institution and are painfully aware that without business from coal, oil, and gas clients to enrich the bottom-line, the very future of their beloved bank was at stake. They pounce on the CEO's second question – on carbon capture, utilization, and storage (CCUS for short although it is also referred to as CCS) and the use of carbon trading platforms to offset emissions – as *the* answer to protect the bank's business model. Both propositions are fraught with uncertainty as the promise and potential of CCUS and carbon offsets has been hyped by boosters, with very little to show by way of results. To ensure that the CEO gets the full picture, with warts and all, let's examine them in turn.

The IEA describes[2] CCUS in simple, cogent terms. "CCUS refers to a suite of technologies that can play an important and diverse role in meeting global energy and climate goals. CCUS involves the capture of CO_2 from large point sources, including power generation or industrial facilities that use either fossil fuels or biomass for fuel." The IEA adds that CO_2 can also be captured directly from the atmosphere. "If not being used on-site, the captured CO_2 is compressed and transported by pipeline, ship, rail, or truck to be used in a range of applications, or injected into deep geological formations

---

[2]About CCUS – Technology report from the IEA, April 2021.

(including depleted oil and gas reservoirs) which trap the CO_2 for permanent storage."

I say this after consuming a pinch of salt. CCUS technology, once scaled and proven viable, will essentially enable the world to produce fossil fuels in perpetuity. Since much of the CO_2 generated by fossil fuels and factories will be captured during the production process itself, it would in theory create the perfect circular economy where the world continues to charge ahead on the carbon industrial economic model with the insurance that global emissions will remain static and thus the trajectory of global warming can be arrested.

It is no surprise that some of the world's largest oil companies have become enthusiastic champions of CCUS. Here is Exxon-Mobil, the same oil company which was a climate denier until very recently wax eloquent about the promise. "CCS is happening today" declared Joe Bloomaert,[3] the company's head of low carbon solutions, "ExxonMobil was the first to capture more than 120 million metric tons of CO_2, which is equivalent to the emissions of more than 25 million cars. And to date we've captured 40% of all human-made CO_2 that's ever been captured. We're now using that expertise to develop technologies to capture CO_2 from natural gas exhaust streams where CO_2 concentrations are more diluted, making the capture process that much more difficult." As context to the company's claim that is has captured 120 million tons of CO_2, it is useful to note that by the company's own disclosure, its Scope 3 emissions in 2020 (from oil and gas production) was around 540 million tons.[4] So, there is a considerable way to go in terms of the American oil major's approach in capturing all of its CO_2 emissions. This still does not resolve the equally pernicious problem of methane leaks from natural gas production and pipelines, which is already causing considerable damage to the planet.

It is no surprise that my own skepticism about the scalability of CCUS is not shared by what can loosely be described as the mining and geological community, validating the position taken by the IEA

---

[3]Helping decarbonize industry with carbon capture and storage – Energy Factor by ExxonMobil, August 12, 2021.
[4]ExxonMobil Energy and Carbon Summary, Scope 3 emissions, April 23, 2021.

and ExxonMobil. "Carbon capture and storage is going to be the only effective way we have in the short-term to prevent our steel industry, coal, cement manufacture, and many other processes from continuing to pour emissions into the atmosphere," said Professor Stuart Haszeldine[5] of Edinburgh University, "If we have any hope of keeping global temperature (increases) down below 2 degrees C then we desperately need to develop ways to capture and store carbon dioxide." It is equally true that emissions from steel, cement, and coal, unlike oil and gas, are proving to be more difficult to abate because of the fragmented nature of manufacturing activity and ownership in these sectors. While the number of major global oil and gas producers are a small elite group, providing CCUS scale and viability, there are literally thousands upon thousands of steel and cement producers all over the world. Abating emissions will require CCUS technology to be deployed on-site and it is arguable whether business will find it commercially feasible to add to their already high production costs.

CCUS skeptics, and there are many powerful voices in this space, believe that the entire focus is a huge distraction, designed to empower CO_2 emitters to pursue a business as usual approach. In a report published in 2021[6] by Friends of the Earth Scotland and Global Witness, two credible interlocutors in the NGO space, the authors assert that instead of financing a technology that can neither develop in time nor make to work as claimed, governments should concentrate on scaling up proven technologies like renewable energy and energy efficiency. "The technology still faces many barriers, would only start to deliver too late, would have to be deployed on a massive scale at a scarcely credible rate and has a history of over-promising and under-delivering," the report notes, bolstering my point of view on the subject. Mark Carney, co-chair of the Glasgow Financial Alliance for Net Zero (GFANZ) and originator of the TCFD proposal also wants a major investment push into renewables, with the financial sector playing an important role in redirecting capital away from fossil fuels. "Given the current

---

[5]Carbon capture is vital to meeting climate goals, scientists tell green critics – The Guardian, January 16, 2021.
[6]Sections of the report were cited in an article in Climate Week, January 9, 2021, which I have drawn from.

limited ambitions and capabilities of traditional energy companies, investors need to redeploy their windfalls to the solutions of the future: wind, solar, hydrogen, nuclear, and other clean energy sources," he writes,[7] "The current spending practices of oil and gas majors are misaligned with the transition to net zero by 2050."

The tussle on the utility of CCUS, between the fossil fuel sector against the skeptics is a healthy development. It injects the right dose of realism into a potentially game changing technology, whose business case to save the planet remains unproven. It is going to take a lot more scientific research and development twinned with independent verification of the claims put forward by the fossil fuel industry for the world to feel comfortable about the emission containment possibilities of CCUS.

Our CEO is unpersuaded with *The Protectors* pitch that CCUS could be one way of continuing to support fossil fuel clients and retain the bank's core business model. He feels that this would be a difficult sell to long-term investors, who were demanding to see a decarbonization plan. The group, somewhat dejected, turns to examining existing carbon offset markets and the promise of building newer marketplaces as the next possible option for the bank to consider. To put it simply, the proposition for carbon offsets is that it establishes an incentive structure for manufacturing companies to manage emissions originating from the factory floor, coal pit, or oil and gas well. These primary emissions can easily be computed in volume and value, the latter being dependent on the still elusive price of carbon, which at the moment varies sharply depending on regional calculations and industry interests. Europe is ground zero to the world's oldest carbon offset markets, the EU Emissions Trading System (ETS) which was established in 2005 and serves on the principle of cap and trade. Very simply, the cap and trade emissions system brings together polluters and climate benefactors (i.e. nonpolluting companies) together to actively manage and trade their emissions. The cap and trade philosophy underlying this allows the EU to set the maximum permissible amount of greenhouse gas emissions by all firms participating in the ETS. The

---

[7]Governments must seize the chance of transform unsustainable energy systems – Mark Carney, Financial Times, August 14, 2022.

ETS issues emission allowances – which enables companies to measure their own annual emissions, which would immediately determine if they exceed a particular year's allowance, a development which would trigger the purchase of allowances in the carbon market.

Let's be clear – the EU ETS and other fragmented market initiatives are working imperfectly because of a singular impediment – agreement on what constitutes a credible price for carbon. The IMF's climate specialist Ian Parry estimates that only about one-fifth of global emissions are covered by pricing programs *and the global average price is only $3 a ton (italics mine)*. This is a significant undershoot because Parry estimates that the world needs a global carbon price of around $75 a ton needed to reduce emissions enough to keep global warming below 2 degrees. "Carbon pricing must be coordinated internationally through a carbon price floor," Parry writes,[8] "Aggressive scaling up of carbon pricing remains difficult when countries are acting unilaterally because they fear for their industrial competitiveness and are uncertain about specific policy actions in other countries." The IMF's recommendation is for the world to have an international carbon price floor, with an initial focus on major emitters in the developed and developing world. A credible carbon price, for example, would help our CEO in determining the full costs of the bank's continued reliance on fossil fuel lending and the horrendous financial burden in mitigating them. As a simple mathematical calculation, the bank's estimated 60 million tons in Scope 3 emissions originating from clients would cost a prohibitive $4.5 billion annually to offset, if the *The Protectors* prevail in retaining the existing client base. This is a gross over-simplification, I agree. The point is even if the argument of *The Protectors* wins the day, there is the small matter of transacting carbon credits in markets which are subscale, fragmented, and lack liquidity and depth, virtues most prized by market practitioners. There is also a fundamental question on the utility of a global price of carbon given sharply differentiated levels of development and distortions in policies across the globe. In that

---

[8] A Proposal to Scale up global carbon pricing – Ian Parry, IMFBlog, International Monetary Fund, June 18, 2021.

sense, the IMF is being aspirational in asking for a carbon price floor since carbon markets themselves lack depth.

As it happens, the ubiquitous Mark Carney made a valiant attempt in scaling carbon markets in 2021, which seems to have stalled over controversy on whether they would genuinely lead to a reduction in global warming. On the face of it, the purpose of the "Taskforce on scaling voluntary carbon markets" is a worthy one. As Bill Gates writes[9] in a foreword to the report, a "robust voluntary carbon market" is one important tool the private sector can use to "address climate change and reach net zero emissions by 2050."

The report itself notes that concrete climate actions by corporations can be grouped into three categories: reduction, reporting, and offsetting GHG emissions that are hard to abate. Building integrity into the carbon price setting process is crucial so that all participants have reasonable assurances that their carbon reduction strategies can be backed up by hard facts. The report also noted that for finance to flow to these GHG emissions avoidance or reduction and removal or sequestration projects, well-functioning voluntary carbon markets will be a critical enabler. "A liquid voluntary carbon market at scale could allow billions of dollars of capital to flow from those making commitments, such as carbon neutral or net zero, into the hands of those with the ability to reduce and remove carbon."

Depending on different price scenarios and their underlying drivers, the market size at stake in 2030 "could be between $5 billion and $30 billion at the lowest end of the spectrum and up to over $50 billion at the highest end." A lot to digest here but it is useful to put the Scope 3 emissions of our case study bank into perspective. At an estimated cost of $4.5 billion in annual carbon offset costs, the activity of a single institution (the bank in our case study) would swamp the system with demand for credits, if the taskforce's estimations of market size are accurate. It is therefore not surprising that the Taskforce itself has had to repurpose its goals because of pungent criticism that offsets traded in the market

---

[9]Foreword by Bill Gates – Report from the Taskforce on Scaling Voluntary Carbon Markets – January 2021.

place will not represent a real reduction in emissions. One contro-versy, unsurprisingly, was over the taskforce's belief that CCUS or carbon sequestration was one possible way for companies to reduce their GHG emissions. As *Bloomberg* reported in March 2022,[10] the taskforce is "repurposing its mission" to tackle the criticism that offsets don't represent real carbon reductions. A slimmed down version of the Taskforce, labeled as the Integrity Council for the Voluntary Carbon Market, will instead focus on the quality of carbon offsets sold, curtailing its earlier ambitions of scaling the size of the market to $100 billion. While the focus on the quality of carbon offsets traded in markets is appropriate, this still leaves our bank CEO without a viable option to hang on to the existing carbon-heavy business model.

The Protectors have had their opportunity to make their case and the odds are clearly stacked against them. It is now up to *The Pragmatists* to articulate their case which seems to be an easy one, including on the bank's own emissions. On curbing the Bank's Scope 1 and 2 emissions, Group A built a credible case for reduc-tions. It calls for a plan for the Bank to locate itself in smarter, more energy efficient buildings across its vast footprint, to go paperless, and to reduce air travel and transport,[11] all goals achievable as the pandemic has reshaped the way of doing business. Many staff are pursuing a hybrid work arrangement, showing up at work one or two days a week and preferring to transact cross-border business via Zoom or Teams rather than expensive air travel. Curtailing Scope 1 and 2 emissions is the easier component of the group's task – dramatically reshaping the business model is going to be a more difficult challenge. The one-sentence recommendation from The Pragmatists in Group B to the CEO was a simple one – double down on sustainable finance (SF).

What exactly is sustainable finance and does it really serve as a panacea for financial institutions attempting to transition away from traditional fossil fuel based business models? The hype in this sector certainly suggests that SF is the next big investment

---

[10]Carney's Bid to Grow Carbon Market Rejigged Amid Controversy – Bloomberg, March 16, 2022.
[11]The purists will quibble that air travel actually belongs to Scope 3 emissions but please bear with me.

opportunity, perhaps on the same scale as the investor mania for
Silicon Valley stocks during the past decade. The European Commission, the global custodian of all definitions concerning the topic,
describes[12] SF as a process of "taking ESG considerations into
account when making investment decisions in the financial sector,
leading to more long-term investments in sustainable economic
activities and projects." In the case of a bank attempting to reba-
lance its lending portfolio away from fossil fuels, the pivot toward
SF would require reducing the existing financial concentration over
time and simultaneously scaling up exposure to the full spectrum of
sustainable finance projects.

International NGOs are an impatient lot and they would
resent my proposition that the rebalancing process should be
time-defined but gradual. The world, rightly or wrongly, is not
ready for an unstable and disruptive energy transition where
banks immediately withdraw from all fossil fuel lending activities and redirect the money toward SF. As we learned in
Chapters 2 and 3, our dependence on fossil fuels is still acute
and it would be unreasonable to expect the transition to happen
immediately. In America, renewables today account for around
20% of total power generation and this percentage is likely to
increase substantially in the years ahead. Similarly, electric
vehicle sales globally in 2021, according to IEA estimates,
touched a new high of 6.6 million "with more now sold each
week than in the whole of 2012." Yet EV sales as a proportion
of total global car sales in the same year accounted to a moderate 10% in the same year (with total car sales estimated at 66
million). For the CEO of the bank desperate to come up with a
new business model, the objectives should be clear. Resting
comfortably on the premise the bank has announced a 2050 net
zero target will not work. Both NGOs and investors are impatient to see tangible change in bank business models and a plan
to pivot to SF should be data dependent rather than rely on high
prose and rhetoric which CEOs spout out whenever they are
placed on the defensive.

---

[12]European Commission – Overview of sustainable finance.

Fortunately for the financial sector, the promise and potential of SF as a distinct asset class is increasingly being realized, bolstering the case for *The Pragmatists*. Data firm Refinitiv estimates[13] that the market for sustainable finance sped past $1 trillion in 2021, "marking a high point in the meteoric rise of a sub-sector that didn't exist a decade ago." Two data points from Refinitiv are startling – sustainable bond issuance is now more than 20-times the size of 2015 and accounts for one-tenth of global capital markets. Meanwhile sustainability-linked loans also "came of age" in 2021 tripling their previous records to hit $717 billion. There is a surge in investor appetite on both sides of the Atlantic for any financial product labeled green, sustainable, or ESG and a huge amount of work still needs to be done by global standard-setters and regulators in setting clear boundaries on what constitutes a genuine green financial product, which is exclusively used for green purposes. Many financial institutions are indeed grappling with investor accusations of greenwashing, i.e., by directing capital into polluting projects under the green label.

We will discuss the risk of greenwashing and how to counter this in the last chapter, but let's return to our CEO and his leadership retreat. It is coming to the end of a very long and intense day of discussion. No one is thinking of retiring to the bar as yet and the CEO is painfully aware that all eyes are on him to deliver a cogent action plan on the tasks ahead. The writing is on the wall. The bank needs to pivot toward sustainable finance under a defined time-table with transparent financial metrics. He whispers to the CFO and head of strategy that the plan should be discussed at the Board during its "strategy week" and then with investors soon after. In the interim, the entire bank should be rallied for this historic task. The CEO is beginning to feel very content, imagining himself delivering the bank's refreshed green strategy in front of a global audience. The head of sustainability taps him on the shoulder. "We need to talk about social issues and supply chains," she says, "The S in ESG."

---

[13]Sustainable finance continues surge in 2021 – Refinitiv Market Insights, February 2, 2022.

6

THE 'S'
OF 'ESG'

THE MERITS OF "WOKE"
CAPITALISM

*What Is Driving Companies to Focus on Social Justice
Issues and Does This Amount to "Woke" Capitalism.*

After taking shots at the late great Milton Friedman in Chapter 2,
it's time to knock *The Economist* newspaper, as it describes itself,
down a notch or two. Now I have been a loyal reader of the
magazine since the 1980s and was even a contributor when I was a

journalist in Indonesia a decade later. The magazine's ideological proclivities are of course well known – liberal in its political leanings and center right in its economics, advocating for capitalism and the globalization pillars of free movement of people, trade, and capital. *The Economist* is not infallible, as its many critics have pointed out, and it has made its fair share of blunders, the most notable of them being its declaration[1] in the late 1990s that we were entering a permanent era of cheap oil.

Into this list one must surely add the magazine's recent special report[2] on ESG. To be fair, the report's initial arguments are something that I agree with. It rightly points out that ESG has "too often" been neither a good measurement tool nor an effective risk management one. "It aims to satisfy so many stakeholders that the information it elicits often bears little resemblance to what a company actually does. It is too imprecise to be a shadow tax on a company's negative externalities. It has created confusion for companies. And it is hard for investors to work out what it means for asset prices." The special report also goes on to suggest that ESG metrics should be "streamlined," which I also agree with, but goes on to make the following wrongheaded recommendation. "It may be better to focus on the E side of ESG, and not the S or the G. In many Anglo-Saxon countries, there are impediments to basing investment decisions on the latter two, given information controls. Regulators, including the SEC, are for now focused exclusively on climate-related disclosures."

Here is some breaking news for *The Economist* and its readers – long before ESG became a thing, the S of ESG was a well-established pillar of corporate governance. Multinational companies, international banks, and multilateral agencies like the World Bank and its affiliates have wrestled with the full portfolio of social impact issues for several decades, with a particular focus on emerging markets. Think of complex supply chains in Asia managed by Apple or garment manufacturers in Bangladesh who supply fast fashion firms with much of their products or an international bank supplying finance to develop palm oil plantations in Indonesia. In each of these cases, the multinational corporation has examined the entire spectrum of

---

[1] Look at for example *The Economist* from March 4, 1999 – Drowning in Oil.
[2] *The Economist* – special report on ESG, July 21, 2022.

environmental and social risks at the last mile of the operation and has come up with a defensible strategy to mitigate them, either by persuading the counterparty to change behaviors or to place tough conditions to access finance or business.

A sign of the imperfect argument put forward by *The Economist* is that a company with a perfect record of achieving net zero emissions, the one metric the magazine appears to prefer, will only be rewarded by investors if the same company also takes social issues seriously. You can't have a company which protects the environment but treats its employees badly and condones human slavery practices in its supply chain. I may be overstating the case but doing away with social metrics altogether will be rewarding companies to perpetuate these bad practices. It is also tone deaf to the times we are living in.

For corporate America, the wakeup call came on May 25, 2020 from a suburb in the mid-western city of Minneapolis. According to official reports, George Floyd, a 46-year-old black man attempted to buy cigarettes at a convenience store with a fake $20 dollar bill. The store employee informed the local police and *The New York Times*[3] reported that 17 minutes after the first squad car arrived at the scene, the following took place. "Mr Floyd was unconscious and pinned beneath three police officers, showing no signs of life." George Floyd was unable to breathe because the lead police officer at the scene, Derek Chauvin who has since been convicted of murder, suffocated him to death by placing his knees on his neck. He was aided and abetted by two accomplices who are also facing jail time. Thanks to the pervasive presence of smart phones, the entire grisly episode soon became prime time viewing for Americans and all over the world.

I have lived on and off in America for over two decades and police impunity, particularly when it comes to treatment of people of color, is considered a given. While the civil rights movement of the 1950s and 1960s galvanized much of America and lead to landmark state protections and legislation, macro and micro inequities, manifested by persistent racial disparities are an uncomfortable hard truth in modern America. What happened after the Floyd murder was a shock – it brought people to the streets all over

---

[3]How George Floyd was killed in police custody – *The New York Times*, May 31, 2020.

America and the world under the unifying banner of "black lives matter." It was an unprecedented social movement which few people saw coming. Perhaps it was the pandemic, which was raging through America when the Floyd murder took place, or it was the zenith of the Trump Presidency which signaled in action and words that it preferred a less diverse, more iniquitous country. I was in D.C. through much of the pandemic and the George Floyd protests had a special feel to them. It brought out the young and the old to the streets in major cities and the mayor of Washington, D.C., the capital of America which also happens to be near black majority had the words "BLACK LIVES MATTER" emblazoned on one of the main streets leading toward the White House. There are many complicated reasons for Donald Trump's defeat in the November 2020 Presidential elections but the BLM movement (and the energy and enthusiasm of young voters it engendered) were certainly a major contributory factor. It is therefore not a surprise that corporate America was forced to rise and show solidarity toward the protest movement even during the early stages.

I have also been on the inside of major public and private sector entities in communication roles and understand how difficult it is to get leadership sign-off on *external* developments which may or may not have a direct impact on the company. The predictable reaction which I have heard from leadership is that the company should stick close to its knitting, i.e., not comment on political or social developments which might damage the company's key external relationships or even endanger its license to operate. The George Floyd murder was a revolution in corporate America because CEOs threw their traditional caution to the winds and come out assertively in support of BLM and the overall agenda of achieving social equity. JP Morgan CEO Jamie Dimon has the reputation of being a hard-nosed corporate leader focused exclusively on business and the bottom-line. In the aftermath of George Floyd's murder, it was a shock to see Dimon take the knee[4]

---

[4]For non-American readers, "taking the knee" originated as a symbol of protest against racial and other inequities. It gained recent prominence when several well-known sports stars kneeled when the national anthem was performed at the start of the game, which some viewed as a sign of dis-respect.

along with other bank employees during a visit[5] to a branch in sub-
urban New York's swish Westchester County.

Countering racial injustice was not a major priority of corporate
America before Floyd's murder but has quickly become one. Here is
The Washington Post[6] with a succinct analysis of the change. "In
new commitments to racial injustice since Floyd's death, the companies are expanding beyond traditional philanthropy, incorporating racial injustice in their regular course of business," the
newspaper commented, "In addition to the external financial
commitments analysed by *The Post*, the companies said they were
diversifying their workforces up to the highest paid C-suite jobs as
well as increasing their purchases of goods and services from
Black-owned businesses." The newspaper added that as of August
23, 2021, well over a year after the Floyd's murder, America's 50
biggest public corporations and their charitable foundations
collectively committed at least $49.5 billion to addressing racial
inequality – **an amount that appears unequaled in sheer scale (text
in bold mine).** Companies making the pledges include JP Morgan's
$28 billion in housing and business loans to Black and Latino
communities, PayPal's $500 million in investment in Black and
Latino financial institutions and venture funds, and Google's $50
million donation to historically Black colleges and universities.
Corporate America's pledges and commitment to address racial
inequality should of course be closely monitored to ensure that the
monies are actually disbursed and are making a difference. These
metrics fall squarely under the social pillar of the ESG umbrella,
which *The Economist* is so anxious to dispose of on the altar of
reducing ESG complexity.

The inevitable question to ask is what would Mr. Friedman
make of this historic shift in corporate attitudes, away from
maximizing shareholder value and profits and tipping the balance
in favor of a more caring, sharing corporation. The answer is surely
that the times have changed and the Friedman doctrine is no longer
fit for purpose. A clear recognition of the doctrine's demise came

---

[5]See *New York Post*, June 5, 2020 – Jamie Dimon drops into Mt. Kisco
Chase branch, takes a knee with staff.
[6]Corporate America's $50 billion promise – *The Washington Post*, August
23, 2021.

from the Business Roundtable (BR), the all-powerful Washington
D.C.-based business lobby group which comprises some of America's leading CEOs, including Jamie Dimon. Well before the
pandemic, BR saw the writing on the wall and redefined the purpose of the corporation to include what we would recognize as ESG
objectives. The five new pillars of BRs commitment to stakeholders
include

- Delivering value to our customers

- Investing in our employees, which includes compensating and
  treating them fairly, supporting them through training and skills
  development, and fostering diversity and inclusion, dignity and
  respect

- Dealing fairly and ethically with our suppliers

- Supporting the communities in which we work. This includes
  respecting the people in our communities and protecting the
  environment "by embracing sustainable practices across our
  business"

- Generating long-term value for shareholders, who provide the
  capital that allows companies to invest, grow, and innovate.

"This new statement better reflects the way corporations can and
should operate today," said Alex Gorsky, executive Chairman of
Johnson and Johnson, "It affirms the essential role corporations can
play in improving our society when CEOs are truly committed to
meeting the needs of all stakeholders." Gorsky is perhaps over-
stating the role that CEOs played in this transformation, given that
corporate America's young and diversified work-force were at the
vanguard of the change. When the protests against the George
Floyd broke out, it was the young staff in companies who agitated
for strong statements from management and for making substantive
financial commitments to deal with racial inequity.
    This approach, labeled "woke capitalism" by its many detrac-
tors, and the most prominent of them being Florida Governor Ron
de Santis, the putative challenger to Donald Trump for the
Republican ticket for the White House in 2024. De Santis has

breathed fire and brimstone against woke capitalists and capitalism, stripping Disney for example of lucrative tax benefits because the company railed against the state's regressive legislation against the LGBT community. Disney was siding with the company's diverse staff in taking this social position and appears prepared to digest the business costs which comes along with this advocacy.

De Santis has also taken aim at ESG investing by requiring the state to "ban" the consideration of "social, political, or ideological interests" when making investment decisions for the state's pension fund. "Corporate power has increasingly been utilized to impose an ideological agenda on the American people through the perversion of financial investment priorities under the euphemistic banners of environmental, social, and corporate governance and diversity, inclusion, and equity," De Santis thundered in a statement announcing the decision. Conservative activists, who are labeling themselves as "anti-woke" warriors, are also pursuing legal action against market platforms for seeking to improve boardroom diversity. In the US state of Louisiana for example, conservative nonprofit groups have sued the Securities and Exchange Commission (SEC) for approving a rule required by the Nasdaq market trading platform for companies to report on how many of their Board members were women, from an under-represented minority of LGBTQ, and explain any lack of diversity. The interesting aspect of the Louisiana legal battle is that many American firms have already embraced Board diversity as an important objective. As a result, "companies are not really waiting to for this to shake out," said a legal expert Jeremiah Williams.[7] They're already responding to the transparency demands. Whatever happens in the court case next, he said, "the train's already left the station" when it comes to ESG investing.

Similarly while the Florida decision by the Governor will impact pension fund managers like BlackRock, it is difficult to see how it could potentially persuade Larry Fink and his cohort of Big Money on Wall Street in returning to the Friedman ethos of making money at all costs. If firms in today's America indeed pursue such a

---

[7]A legal challenge from the right on boardroom transparency – DealBook, *The New York Times*, August 30, 2022.

mercantilist approach, they will find it difficult to retain and attract talent, and build brand loyalty with a customer base which is increasingly focused on social issues. Abortion rights has also emerged as a new battleground between conservative America and big business following the Supreme Court's June 2022 ruling striking out constitutional protections for women seeking abortion. As states dominated by Republicans have sought to introduce outright bans and to criminalize those who seek cross-border access. Confluence Philanthropy, a network of investment managers focused on sustainability, has described abortion as the "newest ESG frontier"[8] and is rallying a coalition of investors to focus attention on this issue. A consequence of the repeal of Constitutional protections are a "weakened talent pool, reduced talent mobility, higher turnover, and an economy weakened by a reduction in the women's labor force participation."

Continental Europe and the UK, given their strong focus on social protection, have been at the vanguard of introducing progressive environmental and social regulations for companies to comply with. As *Reuters* reported,[9] "a gap is emerging and growing" between ESG rules from European regulators and those in the United States. The differences come not only from the volume of new regulations from EU authorities, but also from a more measured less prescriptive approach from US agencies, notably the SEC.

The substantive difference between the two regulatory approaches is that major companies in the US are charging ahead with socially progressive policies and not waiting for the regulatory community to catch up. It is a moot point whether ESG regulation in America will achieve the depth and breadth of what is being envisaged in the EU or indeed it should due to the sharp differences in political philosophy and ethos. In May 2022, the SEC put out a 505 page consultation document to consider amendments "to rules and reporting forms to promote consistent, comparable, and reliable information for investors concerning funds' and advisors'

---

[8]The Newest ESG Frontier: Reproductive Rights at the corporate level – a report on Confluence's 5th Annual Advisors Forum, June 16, 2022.
[9]ESG gap widens: EU rules become more prescriptive as US proposals wait in the wings – Reuters, June 1, 2022.

incorporation of ESG factors." The consultation document was preceded with the SEC's climate disclosure proposal which is aimed at increasing transparency of listed companies on how they are reducing their carbon emissions. Both proposals have been met with hostility in Congress and the US Chamber of Commerce is suing the SEC for regulatory overreach and to prevent the rules to come into force. Given the power of vested interest and business lobbies in America, it is all but certain that the SEC proposals will be significantly diluted on their way to becoming law. However, societal expectations are racing ahead and will force American companies to remain at the cutting edge of staying "woke," much to the annoyance of its many detractors.

In contrast, European regulators have been promiscuous in putting forward ESG regulations, which will become mandatory for listed companies across the EU to implement. Two examples illustrate this trend. The European Council, the EU's governing body adopted the Corporate Sustainability and Reporting Directive (CSRD), a new requirement that all large companies should publish regular reports on their environmental and social activities. "The EU law requires certain large companies to disclose information on the way they operate and manage social and environmental challenges," *Reuters* reported. Another EU-inspired initiative is to integrate social issues into the EU Sustainability Taxonomy, highlighted in an earlier chapter. Rating firm Moody's,[10] which participated in the scoping exercise (as part of the Platform on Sustainable Finance) proposed a detailed framework centered around social objectives. The most "common social controversies" identified by the group include the following:

- Human rights, social, and economic development

- Health and safety

- Product safety

- Remuneration

---

[10]A future EU Social Taxonomy: addressing rising focus on social issues – Moody's, April 26, 2022.

- Social dialogue

- Non-discrimination and diversity

- Societal impact of company's product and services

- Working hours.

"By guiding companies and investors to reduce their negative social impact, respect human rights, and provide access to goods and services for communities, we expect the proposed social taxonomy to facilitate an increase in capital flows toward socially impactful assets, and to help investors appropriately price social risk factors into capital allocation decisions," the Moody's analysis concludes. The proposed EU social taxonomy, if it comes into effect, mirrors the five pillars identified by the Business Roundtable in America as their organizing principle for its membership. The United Kingdom, which no longer follows EU law after Brexit, is attempting to tread its own path in introducing environmental and social regulation with the dual and sometimes conflicting objective of retaining London's status as a major global financial center (which would require lighter touch regulation) and to keep pace with European and American regulation on progressive ESG issues (which will force the country to mimic EU laws and regulations). In my view, the UK's Modern Slavery Act, which was passed into law in 2015 is an excellent example where the country can demonstrate global leadership. The simple objective of the law is to discourage UK domiciled companies from indulging in modern slavery and human trafficking practices both within and outside the country. The scope of the law is global because boards of major listed companies, for example, have to sign on to a statement in the annual report each year that they have taken all reasonable steps to prevent human trafficking and modern slavery in their supply chains. While the UK leads in curbing such social ills, the City simultaneously has a disgraceful record as an enabler and facilitator of global money laundering and corrupt practices, as evidenced by the simple metric that London is home to some of the world's shadiest billionaires and their capital.

A broader commentary about differing American and European regulatory approaches on social issues will also yield the conclusion that while racial disparities persist, America has done a significantly better job in integrating immigrants to the fabric of American society (and the American dream) compared with anything in the EU or the UK. One metric to demonstrate the American system's superiority (at least in boosting diversity at all levels) is to look at the number of CEOs with immigrant roots. The list of Fortune 500 companies run by immigrants include the likes of Microsoft, Google, IBM, Novartis, Fedex, Zoom, Pfizer, Moderna, and Starbucks. There is nothing comparable to this in the EU, where first and second generation immigrants still struggle to integrate themselves into the mainstream of society. The UK has done a better job than the EU as evidenced by the rise of emerging political leaders from South Asia as one example. Although the City itself is more diverse than it has ever been, with more women and people of color in leadership positions, it remains a bastion of white privilege.

In this sense, Europe and the UK urgently need prescriptive and detailed social reform and social regulation for companies compared with the US. Which is why I will be using the five pillars articulated by the Business Roundtable as my organizing principle to assess how companies on both sides are addressing social issues and the metrics which should go with these objectives. To quickly recap the BR pillars include a focus on delivering value to the consumer, investing in employees/boosting diversity, dealing fairly with suppliers, supporting the communities where business operates, and generating long-term value for shareholders. We will leave out the last metric, shareholder value, because it is self-explanatory and has been dealt with at length elsewhere in the book. To make this exercise more interesting, I will assign a score for America and EU/UK on how they are faring on each of the pillars.

CONSUMER PROTECTION

The focus on the consumer first. The rise of the modern corporation has been accompanied by unprecedented concentration of monopoly power in the hands of a few giant entities. Across both sides of the

Atlantic, regulators have had to contend with the full negative impact of corporate behaviors in industries prone to concentration of power – technology and finance being the most egregious. Google, for example, not only leads in search in the US but across the world where its monopoly power has granted it with sweeping access to customer data. Similarly, the global investment management industry is dominated by an elite group comprising BlackRock, Vanguard, Fidelity, Abrdn, and Allianz and the barriers to entry are prohibitive.

Nevertheless, investors have an edge over consumers because of the existence of strong investor protection laws in the US and Europe. The hesitation and caution expressed by financial regulators in approving crypto products is illustrative of this trend. However, no such guardrails exist on the consumer protection side in America. A consumer typically purchases goods and services from massive oligopolies in every sector and these businesses have little interest in protecting consumer rights. Anyone who has to get on the phone with a call center in America to complain about a product will understand what I am talking about. The wait is interminable, compared with say the UK where the call is always answered promptly by a real person. Commitments made by American companies about fair treatment to customers should be discounted because concentration of market power provides them with the ability to ignore regular customer complaints. Social media, Twitter in particular, has emerged as a powerful chancel for customers to express their grievance against a company, who are forced to respond in real time and address the problem as insurance against the tweet going viral.

There are significantly stronger consumer protections in Europe and the UK, as illustrated by the anti-monopoly actions taken by the European Commission (EC) against America's Big Tech firms. Margarethe Vestager is not a household name even in Europe but she is well-known across Silicon Valley and regarded with fear and loathing. As the EC's all powerful Competition Commissioner, Vestager has taken aim at Google, Apple, and other Big Tech firms for anti-competitive behavior and extracted huge fines. "Technology is, in many respects, an enabler for an open, transparent society," she told

Wired magazine.[11] "But it's also an enabler for supervision for a completely unforeseen degree. And for commercialising personal space to an unforeseen degree." The article added that the "invisible hand" of Silicon Valley – the nudging "swarm" of algorithmically filtered data, pushing everything from travel routes to news stories – appears to her intrusive and dehumanizing. "I know what I need. I don't want people to tell me what I need," she said.

ON CONSUMER PROTECTION – THE SCORE IS AS FOLLOWS

Europe/UK – 1, America – 0

Developing metrics for treating customers fairly (TCF) are fairly well-advanced in Europe and America. In terms of outcomes, investors in theory should be rewarding European rather than American companies with a price premium for their superior consumer protection laws. The fact that this is not happening or difficult to discern exemplifies the complexity of ESG as an asset class.

Diversity and Inclusion

The second BR pillar is focused on investing in employees, which includes compensating and training them fairly, supporting them through training skills and development, and fostering diversity and inclusion, dignity and respect. This is quite a mouthful but as I highlighted before, America has done a much better job compared with the Europe and UK in integrating educated and qualified immigrants and providing them with a platform to excel in knowledge-based industries. However, this is not a uniformly positive story because women have struggled to make it to the higher echelons at Silicon Valley or Wall Street. The profile of a typical Silicon Valley executive is a self-absorbed tech bro who

---

[11]Europe versus Silicon Valley: behind enemy lines with the woman deciding Google's fate – Wired, June 27, 2017.

thrives in developing complex algorithms to "change the world," struggles to connect with peers and subordinates, and is blissfully oblivious to what is required of him as a leader and a manager. Unsurprisingly, the ranks of Silicon Valley C-suites with women and people of color (besides the ubiquitous Indian and Chinese) are scarce. Corporate America overall is talking the diversity and inclusion talk, but it is going to be a long while before anyone can declare victory.

One example is the proliferation of diversity and inclusion (D & I) training programs which have become pervasive in corporations. Writing in *Forbes*,[12] Mohammad Anwar notes that D & I programs are widespread in corporate America, but there's a problem: "They're often ineffective at actually creating better environments for employees. These programs allow companies to check the D & I box, but they fail at their most basic objective of changing people's behaviors to be more inclusive." Anwar adds that the "cold, calculated truth" is that many D & I programs aren't implemented with employees' best interests in mind – they're made to avoid lawsuits." Provocative as this comment may be, it is indicative of the perils in believing in some of the social metrics published by major corporations. On D & I, for example, companies usually disclose the number of staff who have undergone training. This is a quantitative metric which is meaningless if not accompanied by data on how exactly the corporation implemented policies to boost voice and representation for women and other minorities.

On paper, Europe and the UK have developed better D & I metrics. Examples include requiring listed companies to disclose the proportion of women in senior ranks of the corporation and on the Board. There are many more prominent women in senior roles in banking and across the FTSE-100 compared with a decade ago. However, companies are still struggling to curb excesses in culture, what in London is described as "laddish behavior," where network of men are prone to subject women to harassment and also limit their career progression by operating as a not-so-secret society for the advancement of men. Over boozy lunches and after-work

---

[12]The Future of Diversity and Inclusion in Corporate America – Mohammad Anwar, Forbes, May 5, 2022.

congregation at the pub, powerful network of men still attempt to dictate the terms under which women can function in the work-place. Swiss bank, UBS, settled a lawsuit in London with a former trainee in 2020 who alleged rape by a former employee. "The Swiss lender agreed to settle the claim after the trainee, who was identified in court documents as Ms A, alleged that UBS failed to protect her and that its investigation of her complaint was flawed. The female graduate, who worked on the trading floor, had also told former UBS Investment Banking head Andrea Orcel of the 'sexualised atmosphere' on the desk," the *Insurance Journal* reported.[13]

Europe and the UK have also done a progressively terrible job in extending the commitment to D & I to include other minorities. The trouble with pursuing D & I disclosure based on a single metric – representation by women, while very important, is that it also ignores people of color. This is not "woke" by any means, a familiar riposte I receive whenever this issue is raised in the City, but a fundamental reflection of a lack of management focus in addressing the root cause of the problem. The travails of Tidjane Thiam, the only black CEO of a major European investment bank (Credit Suisse) until he stepped down in early 2020, are well documented in media. While I am not seeking to absolve Thiam of the many management missteps during his controversial tenure, there has been sufficient coverage of the many micro-inequities and racist behavior which he faced. One notable example is the party held in Zurich to celebrate the 60th birthday of then bank chairman Urs Rohner. *The New York Times* reported[14] that Thiam was the only black guest at the party, not surprising given the rarity of black people at the top rungs of banking in Europe. "Mr Thiam watched as a Black performer came onstage dressed as a janitor and began to dance to music while sweeping the floor. Mr Thiam excused himself and left the room." Credit Suisse subsequently issued a public apology to Thiam "for any offence caused." In addressing diversity and inclusion, both American and European companies should be addressing the pipeline problem, i.e., not enough qualified

---

[13]UBS Settles Lawsuit with former trainee who alleged rape by senior employee – *Insurance Journal*, June 29, 2020.
[14]The Short Tenure and Abrupt Ouster of Banking's Sole Black CEO – *The New York Times*, October 3, 2020.

women and other minorities are pursuing an education which would provide them with the ability to access jobs in the corporate world. This also calls for greater focus and investment in on-the-job training programs.

ON DIVERSITY AND INCLUSION, THE SCORE IS AS FOLLOWS

Europe – 0, America – 1

In terms of metrics, quantitative measures like the number of minorities in senior positions are helpful but incomplete. To attract SRI investors (socially responsible investing) to put money in companies with a stellar track record in D & I, for example, specific disclosure of the company's strategy to build a truly diverse work-force will be needed.

Supply Chains

The third BR pillar is dealing fairly and ethically with suppliers. While corporations have the internal levers to deal with consumer protection and in boosting diversity and inclusion, there are multiple third parties involved in the management of complex supply chains. If you are in fast fashion or manufacturing widgets in different parts of the world, there is a high probability that you will have to manage suppliers in multiple countries – producing garments in sweat shops in Bangladesh or building components for the Apple iPhone for final assembly in China. Supply chain management has become a prime "S" issue in ESG because of a host of human rights and ethical concerns.

Let's take garment manufacturing in Bangladesh as an example. In November 2012 and December 2013, Bangladesh witnessed two devastating work-place tragedies – a fire at the Tazreen garment factory which killed 111 people and the collapse of the Rana Plaza factory building which killed over 1,000. Garment exports are critically important for Bangladesh's economy accounting for nearly 10% of GDP. It is a driver of economic growth and opportunity and some of the world's largest fast fashion brands source supplies from the country. Yet the horrific building collapses, which highlighted abysmal working conditions under which garments are stitched together for sale on high streets all over the world, placed fast fashion firms on the defensive. "The Rana Plaza tragedy focused the world's attention on Bangladesh's garment industry, which has made women their family bread-winners and been an enormous life-line for many people," Human Rights Watch said in a report[15] on the fifth anniversary of the tragedy in 2018, "But these gains have often come at an enormous cost to workers. At the time of the tragedy, few workers received fair wages, fair and decent working conditions, the right to unionise without retribution, and – as Rana Plaza has showed us – to have safe working conditions." Lest you think that workers elsewhere in Asia, employed for example to manufacture sophisticated electronics, enjoy better working conditions, there are any number reports by human rights groups to disabuse you of the notion.

While multinational companies and international banks have to manage a spectrum of risks in their operations, the ones originating from supply chains has risen in prominence in recent years. The question is how these complex risks should be managed. An additional layer of complexity which companies have to contend with is the local regulatory environment where the global company operates in. Bangladesh had lax factory building standards and health and safety rules before the Tazreen and Rana Plaza episodes. The fast fashion companies sourcing garments from these operations insist that all suppliers have to comply with their global code of conduct, an elaborate set of rules and requirements developed at head office by well-meaning ESG specialists. However, the unfortunate reality is that these rules and requirements are often enforced in the breach as reports from NGOs about third-party labor practices routinely highlight. As I have seen first-hand, the rules and regulation governing supply chain management has become a massive ticking-the-box

---

[15] "Remember Rana Plaza: Bangladesh's Garment Workers Still Need Better Protections" – Human Rights Watch, April 23, 2018. I have also drawn from research conducted for my previous book: "Has Asia Lost it? Dynamic Past, Turbulent Future," published in 2021.

exercise for companies, with glowing prose in annual reports and investor presentations. I have some sympathy for companies which contend that their presence in Bangladesh and in other developing countries represent a force for good – by creating employment opportunities and building the foundations of economic growth. At the same time, looking the other way when suppliers don't enforce their tough standards exposes these companies to accusations that they are in the country only for the low production costs. An enlightened approach would require companies to be more realistic in their assessments about social issues in the markets they operate in.

ON SUPPLY CHAINS, THE SCORE IS AS FOLLOWS

Europe – 0; America – 0

Supply chain metrics are a mix of qualitative and quantitative measures, combined with regular audits of how the company is managing risks.

Social Impact

This BR pillar spells out that business should support the communities in which they work. This includes respecting people in our communities and respecting the environment "by embracing sustainable practices across our business." There are many dimensions to this issue and I will focus on one important element – how can companies measure the social impact of their operations and know for sure that they are a force for good? Put this question to a CEO and you are likely to get the following, entirely predictable responses:

- *We create lots of jobs in the country*

- *We pay lots of taxes*

- *We have a CSR program and plants lots of trees*

Each of these propositions are worth exploring. It is an established fact that multinational corporations are huge job creators in the markets they operate in. Tech major Apple, for example, has disclosed that it supports "more than 5 million jobs in China through its local companies, research and development centers, local suppliers, and third-party mobile application developers on its App Store."[16] This is an impressive number by any yardstick but what is usually left unsaid by companies like Apple is the enormous economic value it derives by operating in a developing market like China. There would be no iPhone or Apple Watch produced at scale if Apple's supplier Foxconn had not stepped in to operate the factories in China on the company's behalf. Apple's multi-trillion dollar market capitalization has been built on these efforts. Frustratingly, there are no economic models to calculate the precise social and economic impact of multinational companies operating in the developing world. There are basic input-output models which conceal rather than reveal the full picture. So the next time a company CEO declares that his or her company is creating thousands of jobs in a particular market, it is useful to pause and ask the actual economic benefit which the corporate is deriving from the process. *Proposed metric: A better econometric model to measure the socio-economic impact of multinational corporations operating in countries, including the benefits it derives.*

Taxes are another frustrating and contentious issue. While multinational companies disclose that they are paying direct and indirect taxes globally, there is enough empirical evidence to suggest that tax evasion has become the norm, rather than the exception. Tax avoidance by multinationals happens in two distinct tiers – at the home country where the company is domiciled and in the many markets where it has operating entities. On their home turf, America's Big Tech majors, for example, have feasted for several years on generous tax incentives, rebates, and creative accounting to pay negligible corporate taxes. This problem is magnified at developing countries, which badly need tax revenue to invest in

<hr>

[16]Apple supports more than 5 million jobs in China, tech giant says – *China Daily*, July 5, 2019.

social and physical infrastructure. Depriving developed and developing countries of corporate taxes is a deeply moral issue. Which is why the OECD agreement, now ratified by many countries, will require multinational corporations to pay a global minimum corporate tax (GMCT) of 15%. This reduces the possibility of a company indulging in creative accounting methods like transfer pricing and tax arbitrage (by, for example, recording revenue and profits in tax havens or low-tax jurisdictions). Much to my surprise, tax compliance by companies has not become a major source of contention in the ESG space and should be considered as a critical metric moving forward. *Proposed metric: list of actual taxes paid at HQ and countries where the company operates in.*

The final point about CSR and planting trees is a particular bug-bear of mine. In my view, the phrase corporate social responsibility, should be banished from corporate discourse because it has become a lazy, defensive shorthand for C-suites who don't want to have a serious conversation about the actual social impact of a corporation. There is nothing fundamentally wrong with corporate philanthropy, as a way of demonstrating the company's caring, sharing side. However, the corporate philanthropy industry has become a complex in itself with specialist consulting firms, philanthropy gurus, and local NGOs feeding off the trough of corporate giving. There is creative accounting deployed here as well, where companies calculate the number of staff hours devoted to volunteering calculated as part of overall giving. This of course provides a misleading picture of the company's actual social impact – planting trees or helping clear waste from a beach over a weekend is a good way to raise staff awareness about the immediate community (and also help with team bonding). But it can never be a substitute for measuring actual social impact, particularly when a corporation is causing real damage to the environment. Increasingly corporate philanthropy efforts should be directed to support the core operations of the company – an international bank focused on lending into small business or driving financial inclusion, for example, rather than blindly following peers into planting tree programs.

ON SOCIAL IMPACT, THE SCORE IS AS FOLLOWS

Europe – 0; America – 0

I have over-run the usual word count in writing this chapter simply because there is a lot to say about how companies are planning and implementing the social pillar of ESG. With better metrics, investors can make informed decisions on which company's social impact offering deserves a price premium or discount. Even without a defined ESG regulatory framework, I believe that the social pillar is going to be an important metric for companies to measure their performance. A crucial enabler will be a company's ability to manage risks and to build a governance culture which rewards debate and transparency, topics we will turn to in our next chapter.

7

THE 'G'
OF 'ESG'

BORED OF DIRECTORS

A Group of Elders Have Oversight Over ESG Risks, Governance, Culture, and Conduct – With Mixed Results.

To be a Director of the modern listed corporation in Europe and America is the perfect sinecure. After serving long years in the corporate trenches as the master of the universe, a majority of corporate titans prefer to remain in the game in retirement. Serving as a Director offers them with the perfect blend of power and rewards, without the mind-bending pressures of a full-time role.

The rewards are not measly either. The Chair of a listed bank in the UK can earn up to £1.2 million a year and his/her counterpart in America will earn less, around $725,000 for the Chair of Citigroup, for example, but much more in stock awards. Not bad for a part-time gig if your business model is 3-6-3, as an old joke about retail bankers has it. You borrow money at 3%, lend it at 6%, and be at the golf course daily by 3 p.m.!

Serving on the Board of a listed company has its perils as well, which we will discuss in this chapter, and it is standard practice for Directors to seek D & O insurance, directors and officers insurance, to protect themselves against regulatory and investor action against corporate malfeasance and other failures on their watch. "D & O insurance reimburses the defense costs incurred by board members, managers, and employees in defending against claims made by shareholders or third parties for alleged wrongdoing," says global insurer Allianz,[1] "D & O insurance also covers monetary damages, settlements, and awards resulting from such claims."

While corporate failures, management mis-steps, and scandals still happen with alarming frequency, I would argue that the former corporate warriors currently resident in the Board room have still not come to grips with what ESG means for their role in providing oversight and in ensuring good governance. In Chapter 1, I had illustrated the typical indifference of aging corporate warriors to the challenge of climate change. A big problem is of course generational – if the typical C-suite CEO or CFO were born in the 1960s, the typical Board Director belongs to an earlier era. With this comes a completely different ethos and philosophy about what the average Director regards as "material" in providing oversight. To be sure, Directors are extremely good in a slew of traditional things expected of them – this includes, analyzing and dissecting a company's financial position, CEO succession planning, providing direction and sign-off on corporate strategy, assessing conventional risks, and in ensuring that the internal audit function is independent and provides a sense-check on the overall management of the company. There are also a number of other new areas, notably ESG, where they struggle to understand the full impact.

---

[1] D & O insurance explained – Allianz, June 2022.

Paula Loop, leader of the Governance Insights Centre of auditing firm PWC published a report in 2019, which highlighted the ESG risk management element of a Board's role. What surprised her the most, she said in an interview,[2] was the "lack of understanding" of what ESG means. "A lot of people automatically go to 'E'. They'll go to the environment. But the 'S' and the 'G' are a little bit harder and more all-encompassing. So it's hard to imagine we have directors and companies that say ESG really isn't relevant to them. It's really not an important data point to them." She adds that, actually, it "should affect" every company because all of them face governance issues. "And social issues, every company has employees. You're going to come across the issues whether or not you're in an environmentally sensitive sector or not," she said. And in a final, scathing indictment, Loop suggests that the "knowledge" of Directors in this field is quite limited. "A lot of Directors' knowledge and understanding of this topic comes from what they hear in the Board room. What the CEO is talking about and telling them about," she concludes.

I must acknowledge that a lot of water has passed under the bridge since the Loop findings of 2019. There has been a greater regulatory and investor attention to Board oversight of ESG issues and formal discussions have increased in frequency and intensity. This is particularly true of Board oversight over environmental issues, where investor pressure and regulatory initiatives such as the TCFD have attracted the requisite Board and management attention. As highlighted in the previous chapter, companies are also becoming more socially aware and have been forced to adjust how they operate and treat staff and suppliers.

At the same time, the flock of Directors serving in the modern listed corporation has fundamentally remained unchanged. This suggests that Boardrooms in Europe and America are still overwhelmingly male, white, and in their sixties or seventies, and backgrounds firmly rooted in the corporate world. Recent efforts to improve gender diversity has come after a considerable lag. CNBC reports[3] that

[2]ESG in the Boardroom: A Q & A with PwC's Paula Loop – FEI Daily, February 14, 2019.
[3]More women in the boardroom could drive higher credit ratings and stock returns for firms – they still hold just 29% of seats – CNBC, March 11, 2022.

women held 29% of corporate Board seats in America and Europe in 2022, up from 24% 2 years, citing data from Moody's Investors Service. "Less than a third of corporate Board seats are now held by women, despite evidence that has shown that gender diversity in Boardrooms can lead to higher credit ratings and improved stock performance."

Overall, there were 13,938 board seats in North American and European companies in 2022, Moody's data shows that the proportion of male Directors fell from 76% in 2020 to 71% in 2022. European Central Bank President Christine Lagarde (and my former boss when she was head of the IMF), has memorably noted that if the storied Wall Street investment bank Lehman Brothers was run by sisters, the outcome would have been possibly different. "As I have said many times, if it had been Lehman Sisters rather than Lehman Brothers, the world might well look a lot different today," she wrote[4] in September 2018, on the tenth anniversary of Lehman's collapse, which triggered the global financial crisis "Greater diversity always sharpens thinking, reducing the potential for groupthink. This very diversity also leads to more prudence, and less reckless decision-making that provoked the crisis."

Using the Lagarde argument for greater gender and other diversity in the management of investment banks, I submit that Boardrooms of corporate America and Europe also need to develop greater expertise on ESG issues by recruiting the actual experts to serve on the Board. As the PWC study from 2019 noted, a lot of Directors' knowledge and understanding of ESG issues comes from what they hear in the Board room and what the CEO is telling them and talking to them about. I have had direct experience of briefing Board members over the years on ESG issues and it is usually an uphill battle. The typical Board member is very smart and numerate, quick to dive into the financials of a company. The same Director, however, struggles to understand why he or she should pay attention to ESG issues. One Chair who was facing investor pressure to come up with a basic ESG plan, told me that he was "outsourcing" the problem to me, the consultant, to finalize the approach and "keep the CEO, Board and investors happy." The Board

---

[4]Lagarde wrote about this in a blog posting at imf.org, which was also referenced by The Guardian, September 5, 2018.

itself was composed of members with serious financial and operational expertise but were singularly incapable of agreeing on what ESG issues were material to the company and needed special attention. It must be said that the current suspicion about the value of ESG metrics and allegations of greenwashing can be squarely blamed on corporate C suites and Boards for failing to address the issue and to rely on non-experts to provide advice and counsel. This is not a plea for greater consulting contracts but for Boards to bring in the actual ESG experts to serve alongside them in the Boardroom.

Even a cursory analysis of Board composition of major listed companies in America and the UK shows that despite the rise in environmental, social, and governance risks, finance experts constitute a dominant majority. I am not underplaying the important role that actual accountants and CFOs play in shepherding the financial ship of a company. But let's take a look at the list of non-executive Directors of BP Plc, a large oil and gas conglomerate and their areas of expertise:

Helge Lund, Chairman – previous roles include CEO of oil company Equinor and BG Group
Amanda Blanc – CEO of Aviva Plc, a large investment fund
Pamela Daley – senior roles at GE, tax specialist
Melody Meyer – former President of Chevron Asia Pacific
Tushar Morzaria – former CFO of Barclays Bank
Paula Rosput Reynolds – former CEO of Duke Energy Power Services
Karen Richardson – senior technology roles
John Sawers – retired British diplomat and former head of MI6
Johannes Teyssen – energy expert

By all accounts, this is an impressive group with the right mix of gender and skillsets, perhaps suited for an earlier era when Big Oil and the City dominated the UK economy. As one of the world's largest oil and gas companies with a huge emissions footprint, BP by its own admission[5] "aims to reduce operational emissions by 50

---

[5]The quote is from the BP website.

percent (from 2019 baseline) by 2030, compared with an aim of 30-35 percent previously." Given the sheer scale and impact of its oil and gas operations on the environment, one would have expected the UK giant to find the space on its Board for at least one genuine climate or social impact expert, to provide real-time perspectives on the accelerating pace of global warming and the role of fossil fuel companies in this process?

The answer is probably in the negative because of two possible reasons. First, BP, like its peers in the listed company space in the UK, must be scared of the disruptive challenge in the Boardroom when someone from a non-financial background – perhaps with scientific knowledge about climate change or a social impact expert – rubs shoulders with what is still the oldest boys club in the world. Second, there is a rigid template set by regulators on who is eligible to serve on Boards and this is heavily biased in favor of those with business and financial skills. When the SEC and the UK FCA makes it mandatory for oil and gas companies to recruit genuine climate or social experts, the industry is likely to follow orders in a hurry. The regulators are playing catch-up in building their own in-house expertise on climate. The American regulator Office of the Comptroller of Currency (OCC) recently made headlines when it announced[6] the appointment of its first Chief Climate Risk Officer "to focus on the development and implementation of climate risk management frameworks for the federal banking system." Until other regulators build their own expertise and require the same of companies they supervise, Boards will be building diversity based on gender and ethnicity, important objectives, but less attention being paid to other parameters like non-financial expertise. I have used BP as an illustrative example and it is by no means the only company on either side of the pond with such a stark non-diverse board. The one exception is mining giant Rio Tinto which in the aftermath of the Juukan disaster appointed two reputed non-financial, non-corporate experts to the Board, including former Western Australian politician Ben Wyatt, who is of Yamatji

[6]OCC Announces Chief Climate Risk Officer – News release from OCC, September 12, 2022.

Aboriginal heritage, and Ngaire Woods, a prominent Oxford academic who is well known in the development community. The Australian arm of global accounting firm BDO, which knows a thing or two about corporate governance, argues[7] that there is a misconception that you must have an in-depth understanding of financial reporting in order to be a Director, this is not the case. "While all directors must understand financial viability – especially in this time of particular uncertainty – diversity in director skills knowledge bases, and commercial backgrounds also play an important role for the Board." BDO adds that the Australian Securities and Investments Commission (ASIC) clearly states that the "general duty of the director is to exercise powers and duties with the care and diligence that a reasonable person would have which includes taking steps to ensure you are properly informed about the financial position of the company and ensuring the company doesn't trade if it is insolvent." The BDO blog goes slightly off-track from thereon because it frets if there are fewer Directors with advanced financial skills. Boards will have to rely on a "handful" of financial experts to look closely at the financial health of the company. Rhetorically, one could ask the same question of Boards of companies which are playing a negative role in climate change but have *no* climate experts, not even a handful to BDO's point, to advice on how to manage decarbonization and the gravest planetary crisis of our times.

In the absence of access to real ESG expertise, how are Boards playing their central role in providing oversight? Recruitment firm SpencerStuart notes[8] that the Board has become a central player in overseeing and integrating ESG risks and opportunities into their own organizations – even "as they rush" to gather the experience and expertise needed to lead in the topic. The firm polled 590 corporate Directors for insights on how Boards are structuring oversight of ESG issues. The results make for interesting reading:

---

[7]Why financial understanding is critical when you're a non-financial director – BDO, March 26, 2020.
[8]Sustainability in the spotlight: Board ESG Oversight and Strategy – SpencerStuart, May 2022.

- A plurality of respondents (43%) said primary ESG oversight is at the full Board level, followed by nominating/governance committee (30%), and ESG/Sustainability committee (15%).

- Despite the "intense focus" on ESG from shareholders and other stakeholders, only a third (33%) of respondents said that their organizations are considering rethinking their structures and practices around ESG.

- The pandemic "accelerated" ESG discussions in the Boardroom. Before the pandemic, about 20% of respondents said they rarely or never discussed ESG. That percentage is now down to 4%.

- ESG goals and metrics are increasingly incorporated into other elements of business; 71% of respondents are incorporating ESG goals and metrics into overall company strategy. Another 52% are incorporating ESG into integrated risk management, 48% into criteria for director appointments, and 46% in executive compensation.

There is good news and bad news in the SpencerStuart findings. It is encouraging to see that primary ESG oversight is at the Board level and not at some nebulous corporate responsibility group which reports into Management, which was the norm until recently. Yet it is distressing to read the second finding that only a minority of companies are reconsidering their structures and practices despite the intense external focus on ESG matters. It is this anomaly or disconnect which possibly explains why companies are rushing to make bold external commitments on reforming their purpose while doing very little on the inside to reconfigure their operations. The result is the growing public cynicism about greenwashing. A striking example is in revamping internal policies and processes, a thorny issue which I encounter in my consulting work with a number of companies. To put it mildly, taking a deep dive into a company's complex internal policies and processes is a task for the foolhardy.

Instinctively, company CEOs recognize that a refresh of purpose, strategy, and ESG frameworks should be accompanied by a complete overhaul of existing policies and processes. If the new objective of the environment department is to source renewable energy to cool or heat the company's HQ or to reduce paper consumption, someone has to take the responsibility for writing the underlying policy which sets these in stone and to revamp any internal processes which may result due to these changes. Much to my horror, I have encountered fierce turf battles as process owners (i.e. departments responsible for a specific process) resist any change because instructions are coming from the new head of sustainability or ESG, a relative newbie who is not the process owner. To make matters worse, no department wants to "own" the company's new climate policy which sets out net zero targets and other wildly ambitious ESG exhortations from the CEO. So unless the Board steps in and says "so let it be written, so let it be done,"[9] nothing gets done in the modern corporation. Which is why Boards are focusing greater attention on the one function in the financial sector which is naturally designed to articulate, manage, and measure ESG and report to the Board – the Risk function.

Risk officers in large financial institutions are a dour, sober lot – very different in temperament and tone compared with the usual asset manager or investment banker. The risk function exists within the formal corporate hierarchy with the Chief Risk Officer (CRO) at the top and is designed to offer independent assessments about a potential investment or transaction and the institution's overall risk profile. Conceivably a bank or asset manager's exposure to fossil fuels should be a top risk priority for the CRO and the Board Risk Committee. Commenting on the role of the CRO in addressing climate financial risk, Maria Turner of search firm Odgers Berndtson cites[10] competitive advantage and business transformation as factors needed in order to embed climate financial risk into the organisation for long-term strategic business positioning. She commented that, "business transformation is required for this with the CRO being heavily involved," making the point that "climate change risk needs to be managed, it's not just a PR exercise." While CROs and banks have certainly gotten

---

[9]Most readers will be unfamiliar with this quote, which was uttered by Yul Brynner playing Rameses II in Cecil B DeMille epic movie "The Ten Commandments."
[10]The role of the CRO in addressing financial climate risk – Odgers Interim, February 26, 2020.

better at the game, there is still a great deal of hesitation about incorporating and integrating ESG risks into the full suite of the risk portfolio. Climate risk was initially regarded by City banks as a "principal uncertainty" rather than a defined risk type, which essentially means that fewer resources would be devoted to the task. TCFD was a truly transformative moment in forcing banks and asset managers to migrate climate risk to a defined risk type and build out staff teams to carry out scenario analysis and risk assessments. With climate and environmental risks getting an uplift due to TCFD, the "S" of ESG has become an orphan because multiple regulatory agencies provide oversight without a consolidated view of the risks.

A fundamental question is even if CROs and the risk function have built in-house climate risk capabilities, what exactly should be the short-and-medium term scenarios they should be exploring. The CRO and the Board risk committee have a central role in defining the institution's climate change approach and setting scenarios with the objective of preventing the stranded asset challenge we discussed in Chapter 5. I want to set out what regulators expect and compare that with the actual capacity of the risk function and Boards to deliver results. The Network for Greening the Financial System (NGFS), which brings together central banks and financial supervisors has published[11] a series of technical documents meant to strengthen regulatory understanding of this issue. While acknowledging that "challenges and shortcomings remain," which have persisted since the original guidance was published in 2020, NGFS has attempted to provide "practical advice" to regulators on using scenario analysis to assess climate risks to the economy and the financial system. The guide itself provides a four-step process, recognizing that the field is still in its infancy. The four steps include:

- Identify objectives and exposures. Scenario analysis is relevant to many objectives of central banks and financial supervisors. It can be used to stress-test financial firms and the financial system, explore structural changes to the economy and/or assess risks to central banks' own portfolios.

---

[11]Guide to climate scenario analysis for central banks and supervisors – NGFS Technical Document, June 2020.

- Choose climate scenarios. NGFS notes that most publicly available climate scenarios were originally designed for policy evaluation and research, and are therefore not entirely appropriate for central banks and supervisors' purposes. Instead the NGFS has worked with academics to come up with "high-level reference scenarios" that can be used for scenario analysis in a comparable way across different jurisdictions.

- Assess economic and financial impacts. Central banks are interested in assessing the impact of climate risks on a wide-ranging set of economic and financial variables. Examples include GDP, inflation, equity and bond prices, loan valuations. This includes risks that arise from different physical and transition outcomes across a wide range of sectors and geographies. One example, the NGFS paper says that methodologies for financial assessment of climate risks are also developing. "A key challenge is obtaining granular enough information on how the scenario would affect economic activity to assess the financial risks."

- The final step in the NGFS guidance is communicating and using results. Communicating the results, and the key assumptions underpinning them will help increase awareness. This may provide a basis for follow-up actions from central banks and supervisors and encourage financial institutions to improve their risk-management practices.

Let's return to the issue of how bank Boards and the CRO might potentially handle climate scenario analysis, following the four-step model suggested by the NGFS. The first challenge is in identifying objectives and exposures, which may appear to be a seemingly innocuous issue which bank officers could access at the press of a button. You are wrong in making that assumption because contrary to what you might read about an institution's fit for purpose risk management model in glossy annual reports, all the information is not easily accessible. I am amused with reading repeated media references to banks owning a treasure trove of customer data, which happens to be true, but it is not all available in a single place. The external narrative about data being the "new oil" and financial institutions serving as custodians of "rivers" of customer information faces grim reality when a risk officer actually attempts to pull together information on the bank's exposure to a specific customer or sector. Unlike Big Tech firms, which have done a superb job in mining customer data, the typical large bank is hopelessly behind the times. Data is stored in several dozen legacy systems, which even the IT department struggles to manage, and also within departmental silos. Assembling all of the climate relevant data-sets into one easy-to-read spreadsheet has consumed institutional budgets and staff resources for the last 3 years. It is no exaggeration to say that many banks simply don't have all of the information to properly assess the full extent of climate risks in their portfolios.

It will require the diligence of the CRO and the Board to ensure that enough material data is gathered which will give the bank an indicative benchmark on the shape and size of fossil fuel exposures and potential risks. A big challenge in setting long-term net zero targets (2050 being the norm) is that the problem could be delegated to future generations who will run the bank or the asset management firm. This is why it is not enough for banks to not only understand the shape of their fossil fuel-dominated balance sheet but also to conduct scenario work on how a changing climate is likely to impact the geographies they operate in and the clients they do business with. This is not rocket science but is proving to be as complex for financial institutions as putting together a booster rocket into space.

Let me illustrate this with a simple example. A large asset manager based in New York has invested in a global portfolio of companies in developed and emerging markets. Assume for a moment that the asset manager puts money into a mix of traditional fossil fuel and green assets. As part of the manager's declared net zero target, it must figure out how to withdraw from fossil fuels and reshape its investment portfolio in non-polluting and green assets. This is the first phase of what regulators are already expecting asset managers and banks to undertake. The second layer is even more complex – the asset manager has exposure to several emerging markets who are at the front-line of climate distress, either from rising ground temperatures or at risk from flooding, which will have a tangible, direct impact on the investment portfolio (since even green companies will be impacted by natural disasters). A detailed climate scenario analysis approved by the asset manager's Board should factor in all of these considerations.

After facing sustained criticism that the alliance was all talk and little substance, GFANZ has swung into action by announcing a series of industry-led initiatives to put some meat into net zero plans announced by members of the grouping. "To cut global emissions in half by 2030 and meet the goal of net zero emissions by 2050, we need to significantly scale up private capital to companies and assets that are enabling the net zero transition," GFANZ Vice Chair Mary Schapiro said, "But without a clear framework for the transition, progress will be difficult to achieve. Filling the gaps of ambitious climate public policies and regulation, GFANZ has developed a global baseline for financial institutions to turn their commitments into immediate action." GFANZ has identified four "essential" approaches – finance the development and scaling of net zero technologies or services to replace high-emitting sources; increase support for companies that are already aligned to a 1.5°C pathway; enable high and low-emitting real-economy companies to align business activity consistent with a 1.5°C pathway for their sector; accelerate managed phaseout of high-emitting assets through early retirement. The GFANZ work plan is similar to other industry-led initiatives such as the Science-based Targets Initiative (SBTI), for which several leading companies have also signed up to and aims to provide a "clearly defined pathway" to reduce GHGs, helping prevent the worst impacts of climate change and future-proof business growth.

When bank chairmen are asked these days about their institution's commitment to ESG or climate change, they reflexively respond by noting that they are a member of the GFANZ or the SBTI, or any of the other alphabet soup of industry initiatives. There is a safety net for signing up to these grand alliances but the question that investors should constantly ask is how the individual institution is advancing progress on these goals and the financial impact. This task is ideally suited for Boards and the important committee which sets compensation for the CEO and the CFO. How realistic is to set CEO compensation based on actual performance of ESG goals? The initial response was one of horror because these goals are primarily non-financial in nature and creating a credible and transparent compensation framework was going to be difficult. The typical Board chair and head of the compensation committee, which is tasked with setting transparent pay and bonus targets for the CEO, are uncomfortable with blending ESG metrics with the traditional black-box which goes into determining pay-outs. The conventional metrics which they rely on is the financial value which the company has achieved under the CEO's watch. The correlation between financial value created and CEO pay has also become distorted because few Boards can say with a straight face that the mind-boggling levels of compensation set for the CEO could be justified.

The Economic Policy Institute estimated[12] in 2021 that CEO pay in America has skyrocketed a staggering 1,322% since 1978 and in 2020 alone, CEOs were paid 351 times as much as a typical worker in 2020. "From 1978 to 2020, CEO pay based on realised compensation grew by 1322 percent far outstripping S & P stock market growth (817 percent) and top 0.1 earnings growth (which was 341 percent between 1978 and 2019, the latest data available). In contrast, compensation of the typical worker grew by just 18 percent from 1978 to 2020." A similar gap has emerged in the UK where banker pay has been a contentious political issue since the 2008 global financial crisis (GFC). Things are different in the EU, where regulators have placed a hard cap on banker bonuses and overall CEO pay is modest compared with their Anglo-Saxon counterparts. However, the issue of including ESG considerations into CEO pay packages is winning broad support in America and Europe, both as appropriate given the sheer scale of what needs to be done on the ESG front, as well as the only metric which could serve as a moderator to out-sized CEO pay increases. Suppose you are the CEO of a major steel manufacturing company which has been repeatedly fined by regulators for poor health and safety practices on the shop floor and for polluting the communities where it operates. At the same time, the steel company is reporting record profits and has become the darling of Wall Street. It is all but

---

[12]CEO Pay has skyrocketed 1,322% since 1978 – Economic Policy Institute, August 10, 2021.

inevitable that the CEO stands to receive handsome rewards with the pollution, health, and safety issues relegated as a minor issue for management.

There is a social dimension to senior executive pay due to rising income inequality in the west, a trend which is likely to accelerate unless aligned with specific ESG goals. The good news, according to Sustainalytics,[13] is that "more and more" companies are recognizing the potential value that linking executive compensation to ESG metrics can provide. The sustainability research and data firm offered five pithy reasons for the increasing use of ESG metrics in setting executive pay:

- Corporate policies that link ESG targets to executive performance have become a clear priority for investors.

- Linking pay to ESG performance can align executive action with corporate strategy.

- With increased scrutiny on corporate ESG risk, tying variable compensation to ESG performance provides an additional tool for firms and boards to hold their executives to account.

- An effective ESG pay-link may enhance financial performance in a number of ways. For example, in terms of enterprise value, there's mounting evidence that ESG-integrated portfolios provide better financial returns than benchmarks, plus improved risk management.

- Large firms are using sustainability-linked compensation to address social concerns.

While the momentum for ESG-linked performance metrics and pay is building, and includes the likes of Apple (where it disclosed that it aims to enhance or decrease executive pay by 10% based on ESG metrics) and even BP, which says that the annual incentive now includes an environmental goal, which has a 20% weighting in the overall pay metric. The profound question is whether Boards will

---

[13]Should Leadership Compensation Be Tied to ESG metrics? Here's Why It Makes Sense – Sustainalytics, June 9, 2022.

shed their timidity, take an expansive view of how their company is impacting society and build financial and nonfinancial metrics determining how senior executives are compensated.

Over a decade ago, Boards could invoke Milton Friedman's mantra and assert that their primary job is to protect shareholder interests. Protecting shareholder interests in today's context would require Boards to step in to areas which are not defined by spreadsheets and profit and loss considerations. Investors (and an important segment of the business community) have changed with the times and Boards are unfortunately leading from behind. As much as the culture and conduct of organizations have to change to adjust to the new realities, the Board itself need to review its own conduct and overall effectiveness. Board effectiveness reviews have become ticking the box exercises for listed companies and ESG issues do not feature in the process. While effectiveness reviews are mandated by regulators, they are usually carried out by ostensibly independent consulting arms of giant auditing firms, creating a direct conflict of interest. Since securing and sustaining business will be top of mind of consulting firms, their "independent" assessments should be taken with a healthy dose of skepticism. Specifically, when the time comes for a Board effectiveness review of the company's ESG stewardship, I hope that this exercise will be carried out by genuine environmental and social impact specialists rather than add to the gravy train of consulting fees accruing to existing firms.

To return to first principles, if CEOs are enamored with building their ESG credentials through rhetoric and aging Boards cannot be the vanguard of change, is there a segment of the staff population who could be counted on to push the envelope. Let's meet the millennial staff who are attempting to transform organizational culture from the inside, with E, S, and G serving as guiding principles.

8

REBELS WITHOUT A PAUSE

*Can Millennials Transform the Hidebound Culture of
Business and Deliver ESG.*

The modern corporation is singularly unprepared to deal with its
newest entrant – disruptive, energetic, moody, needy, and socially
committed millennial staff? Successive generations of corporate
masters of the universe, who have risen up the corporate ladder
have learned to adjust and adapt to the eccentricities and demands
of their employers. Not this group. The corporation has been
likened to a lumbering beast, even a dinosaur, slow to adapt and
self-absorbed, with a typically dysfunctional work environment
built on the mantra which is also the scariest sentence in the English
language – THIS IS THE WAY WE DO THINGS! The millennial
generation, i.e., those born between 1981 and 1996 and their
successor Gen-Z, has come of age to fill the middle and junior ranks
of corporate America, Europe, and around the world. They come
with their preconceived notions about work and have their own
ammunition to respond to dictatorial corporate directives – plenty
of exclamation marks, emojis, and distress that their superiors are a
bunch of old men who are best met with the riposte "Okay
Boomer." As intergenerational battles go, this is likely to be the
most profound in shaping the corporation of the future. Will
companies be responsible stewards of the environment and in
nurturing positive social impact or just pay lip-service which is the
norm at the moment?

Before we get to these meaty issues, let's take a brief rewind to the past, circa 1980s, to provide some perspective on why the millennials may be right in their preoccupations with social and political issues and their suspicion of elders. When my generation came of age, Boomers II as we are referred to, the carefree era of free love, rebellion, and Woodstock was long past and we were a pragmatic group with low enthusiasm to reshape the world. Indeed, we were the Miltonnial generation – raised on the Milton Friedman ethos of the primacy of the corporation, shareholder value, and profit maximization. We entered the work-place with expectations of secure, life-long employment and jobs and opportunities were aplenty. Even in India, where I grew up and held my first few jobs, opportunities for those with a college degree were significantly more even in a closed economy. I chose my words carefully here – we were grateful for having the job and did not question or reflect on the rigidly hierarchical organizational culture which we worked in. This was the Miltonnial generations' primary mode of thinking or the lack of it. The boss was always right and we all had to adhere to "the process," the strange internal ways in which the organization transacted with itself and with the world. We embraced this as the only way to do things and were awestruck by all things Japanese – the obeisance of the humble salaryman to his superiors and the ridiculous success of mega corporations like Sony and Toyota – which the management consulting industry documented in obsessive, breath-taking detail. In short, we were spine and voice challenged as we sailed along merrily in the heady days of the globalization era, where trade, investment, and free enterprise flourished and organizational culture, with valedictory tomes from Peter Drucker and Tom Peters, numbed us into believing that this was Utopia.

We were also a self-satisfied bunch. As a business journalist in Singapore in the 1990s, I vividly remember the corporate reaction to the first United Nations Climate Summit at Rio in 1992. The zeitgeist was indifference and chopping down trees and treating workers badly were shrugged away in the name of progress. A popular television spot in Hong Kong in the early 1990s showed a well-heeled corporate-type buying an entire island from a befuddled seller who asks him what possible use the island would be to him.

"Chopsticks" the corporate type briskly replies, implying that would tear down all of the trees on the island to supply chopsticks to hungry diners. Such an advertisement running today would be "canceled" instantly, with outrage over outrage piled over social media, as is already happening for a number of storied corporate brands. Our generation did have our own millennials, in spirit at least – a caring sharing, and easily agitated group which rallied and mobilized the public against the actions of Big Business and governments. They were (and are) international and grassroots NGOs who ran successful campaigns to keep business in check.

The most spectacular example of NGO activism against a major American corporation was the campaign against Nike, which sourced much of its shoes from East Asia – initially from Korea and Taiwan, where domestic labor and social protections were strong, and eventually in South East Asia, where the legal and legislative framework was extremely weak and the company was able to get away by paying hyper-low wages with limited benefits. In today's context, this would fit into the "S" pillar of ESG. As an interesting paper from Elvira Oveido illustrates,[1] the "amount of money" that Nike was saving by not paying their factory workers fair or living wages was widely regarded to be one of the main reasons why the company's popularity and revenue steadily surged in the early 1990s. "With the money Nike was saving from minimising their manufacturing and overseas employee wages, Nike turned their business model into one that used those saved costs for aggressive marketing campaigns, which included highly visible and widespread sponsorships with sports teams, athletes and celebrities." I recall many of my generation being mesmerized by Nike's advertising campaign during the Barcelona Olympics in 1992, where basketball star Michael Jordan was the most prominent celebrity endorsing Nike's products and urging us to *just do it*, as the company's slogan promised.

As the Oveido paper highlights, when an American labor activist Jeffrey Ballinger published a report highlighting shockingly low wage and poor working conditions inside one of Nike's manufacturing

---

[1] A Look Into Voluntary Nongovernmental organization (NGO) certifications on labor conditions in international, trade law: Nike, A Case Study – Elvira Oveido, South Carolina Journal of International Law and Business, Volume 18, Issue 2, 2022.

facilities in Indonesia, the impact was immediate. Even by the standards of that era, the report was explosive as Ballinger cited the example of an Indonesian female worker who was getting paid just 14 cents an hour, which was even well below Indonesian minimum wages at the time. I was a journalist in Indonesia in the mid-1990s and shoe manufacturers, often owned by Korean firms, were ubiquitous all over Jakarta. They proudly displayed shoe wear brands they represented – Nike, Adidas, Reebok – but their operations had a darker side in suppressing worker wages and rights. "Ballinger drew attention to the fact that while Nike[2] made $3 billion in revenues in 1991 alone, $200 million dollars of which went toward funding Michael Jordan's sponsorship the following year. Nike was complacent in paying their overseas workers abysmal wages in similarly abysmal working conditions," Oveido writes. I remember that there was some outrage expressed by the rich world's consumers to the report and some may even have walked away from the brand because of the negative media attention. But this was nothing quite on the scale of what the millennial generation of today can achieve on short order. "Now, collective voices spreading like digital wildfire can sway public opinion," a 2021 report from Porter Novelli highlights,[3] "One misstep or wrong word from a person, a celebrity, or a brand can put that entity in a social media maelstrom – when mutual disapproval puts that entity on the outs. It's a phenomenon that has come to be known as "cancel culture"."

Now there is an entire industry out there which has derided cancel culture and so-called woke capitalism, as I have noted in previous chapters. In the American context, there is a fair amount of mud-slinging against the millennial generation for being too politically correct, too sensitive, and too quick to cancel. They are the butt of jokes from late-night talk show hosts, Bill Maher notably had this to say about millennials on one of his shows[4] recently. "You think my generation is an eye-roll," Maher declared on camera, "Let me tell you

---

[2]Ben Affleck has just made a movie, "Air", which is an account of how Nike signed Michael Jordan. No mention of course of poor worker conditions which was a building block for success.
[3]Porter Novelli's 2021 Business of Cancel Culture Study – January 25, 2021.
[4]From Real Time with Bill Maher, New Rules segment, aired on HBO on June 17, 2022.

about the younger generation. Your sense of entitlement is legendary," going on to criticize the millennials for their low attention span and work-ethic. Maher has also railed against the new generation's refusal to support the principle of free speech by "canceling" anyone deemed to have contentious views. American campuses have become a hot-bed of millennial cancellation activity as a huge number of prominent luminaries have been forced to withdraw their speaking engagements on campus because of the student rebellion against their views, past and present.

I am greatly amused with the derision and abuse subjected to millennials from an older generation of entitled Boomers, whose own background and political and economic context radically differ from the challenges faced by youth today. The Boomer generation's signature legacy is a world with sharp racial and income divides, a more uncertain and fluid job market, tense geopolitics from the rise of China, and a planet which is teetering from global warming and climate devastation. "A young college graduate, having faithfully followed the American path of hard work and achievement, might find herself in a position akin to a homeowner with negative equity: in possession of an asset that is worth much less than what she owns," writes[5] the incredibly talented millennial Jia Tolentino in *The New Yorker*, "In these conditions, I suspect, the idea of specialness looks like a reward but mostly functions as punishment, bestowing on us the idea that there is no good way of existing other than constantly generating returns."

The point about the futility of generating returns resonates with millennials, particularly in the face of constant media attention, in particular about how this generation is posed to inherit significantly more wealth than that of their parents' generation. "Millennials may struggle to join the housing market and be laden with debt for their education but they eventually stand to inherit much more than their parents or grandparents ever did," the *Financial Times* said,[6] citing a study from London's Resolution Foundation. The study found that the money passed on through inheritance each year has doubled over

<hr/>

[5]Where Millennials Came From and why we insist on blaming them for it – Jia Tolentino, The New Yorker, November 27, 2017.
[6]UK Millennials fall behind on living standards – Financial Times, February 20, 2018.

the past two decades – and will more than double again over the next 20 years as wealthy baby boomers pass away. This inheritance bounty is not necessarily an easy path for millennials. "However, the think-tank said inheritances were likely to arrive too late to help many millennials get on the housing ladder during their child-rearing years. The think-tank's estimate – based on the age and life expectancy of parents – is that the average age to inherit will be 61." Working in the City in London, I had an opportunity to interact with and indeed supervise many millennials on the team. Their career aspirations and objectives, to put it mildly, were radically different from my generation, which explains much of the angst and frustration expressed by the elders. What corporate bosses do not realize that this is an experiential generation, which loathes formality, rigid hierarchy, and crushing corporate process. At the same time, it is completely untrue that the incoming generation into the work-place is less passionate about their careers or the corporation they happen to be working in. So boomers and Gen-Xers reading this book, who happen to supervise millennials, please repeat after me the following five commandments:

Millennials on my team have a different work ethos from mine

They are more committed to social and environmental issues, but that is good.

I shalt not judge millennials by the standards set by my superiors when I joined the work place in … (inset year of first job).

I shalt not be around when global warming reaches its peak so I will defer to my juniors on the urgency of dealing with climate change.

I shall be open-minded when juniors challenge me on my outdated thinking on racial and gender equity.

The problem with millennials in the work-place is mainly a problem of an older generation of middle and senior management failing to adjust to the new realities. Unlike the ossified generation still dominating corporate C-suites in America and Europe, the millennial generation instinctively understands ESG and don't consider it to be notorious at all. As *Forbes* magazine points out,[7] if you Google "millennial,", you'll find a flood of articles about how to manage them. "However, despite their stereotypical bad rap, millennials want to connect with their organisations and do great things with them." The magazine then goes on to provide four sensible suggestions on how to motivate and manage the incoming flood of young people into the workplace.

- *Recognize their motivation:* Millennials have "different work desires' from previous generations. They don't want to work extra hours, but that's not to be construed as lazy. Many studies highlight that millennials are driven by a desire to make a positive difference to the world. Understandably, since they are so socially focused, millennials often find it hard to see how their work contributes positively to the company and the society at large. Much of this has to do with communications and management. Companies have one-size-fits-all induction programs for staff, which I have attended *ad nauseum*, and very little attention is paid to the design of these programs which should be aligned with the aspirations and motivations of young people. "Companies can help resolve this issue with millennials by clearly outlining the purpose and impact of their job roles in relation to company values," *Forbes* suggests.

- *Create opportunities for growth:* Millennials are "known" – rightly or wrongly – as job hoppers. But what they want and need from a job is an opportunity to connect and grow while feeling like an organic part of the company. *Forbes* says that this is a "highly attractive quality" that organizations can offer to attract and retain millennials. "You can offer to help them identify and develop new skills linked to the mission of the company. What's more, doing this while giving them autonomy – and monitoring the inherent risk from afar – will keep them stimulated, engaged, and productive."

- *Promote work-life balance:* In case you have not noticed, millennials work differently from past generations. The pandemic,

---

[7]Managing Millennials in the Workplace – Laura Berger, Forbes, February 13, 2020.

while crushingly tragic on most fronts, was a liberating moment for millennials because it unshackled them from the going-to-office experience. Many companies in America and Europe are requiring all staff to show up at the work place and are facing a great deal of resistance as a result. Elon Musk famously gave an ultimatum[8] to Tesla staff to show up at work, requiring them to be in the office for a minimum of 40 hours per week "or depart Tesla." For companies which are flexible in their approach and allow staff to WFH (work from home in case you did not know), monitoring and motivating them presents new challenges. *Forbes* recommends micro motivation measures like introducing better communication tools and periodic face-to-face interactions as a way of energizing young staff.

- *Go with the wave of change:* The final recommendation from *Forbes* essentially asks older managers to go with the flow (GWTF). "There are many things today that are changing the work force, from the evolution of technology to the styles and attitudes of the people who use it. The older mentality must adapt to the new as it becomes the mainstream."

Management gurus at the MIT Sloan Management Review believe that the pandemic has been a great accelerator in reshaping corporate perceptions about the traditional work place. But is has not been the only factor. "It has also been a time of political divisiveness, social unrest driven by racial inequality, and ongoing digital disruption to name a few," the authors argue,[9] "Over the next few months, leaders would be well served by taking the opportunity to learn how to apply the innovations and advances implemented in recent months and developing an approach for ongoing workplace reinvention that is more resilient to all types of disruption." Maximizing the benefits of both remote and what the authors describe as "colocated" work ideally works in favor of millennials who chafe against corporate requirements for 9–5 presence at the work place. "The workplace, work force, and work

---

[8]The Musk quote is drawn from a report in Bloomberg – June 1, 2022.
[9]Redesigning the post-pandemic workplace – MIT Sloan Management Review, February 10, 2021.

of the future will be fundamentally different as a result of the pandemic," the authors conclude "The gradual emergence from this disruption provides an unprecedented opportunity to explore and experiment. Leaders must learn to continually reinvent the future of work, and now is the time to begin discovering how to bring that future about."

These are lofty words from the gurus at MIT Sloan and they are right in asserting that the work place is facing multiple disruptions, not only from twenty somethings. In the context of the topic of this book, the final recommendation from *Forbes*, suggesting that company managements GWTF, not just about WFH but the entire spectrum of managing a young work force at a time of disruptive change is the most difficult of them all. We met a CEO in the previous chapter who received a quick education about all things ESG from his children, who were fretting about the brand and reputation of the company their Dad managed and how to deal with awkward conversations about the same from friends. A Gallup poll in America found that 70% of Americans in the 18–34 age group are worried about the impacts of global warming, while among those 55 and older the rate is just 56%. The typical CEO's calendar is an immovable feast of business travel, top team meetings, business and budget reviews, schmoozing with clients, and some outreach with staff. It is highly probable that a CEO in his or her 50s, with Silicon Valley being a rare exception, is only likely to encounter peers in the same age bracket during business interactions in a typical year. The business class lounges and cabins of aircraft are filled to be brim by these aging corporate leaders, further creating bubble conditions.

Listening does not come easy for the typical CEO, particularly listening to perspectives from younger staff who are likely to demonstrate a lack of political sophistication about the way the world works. How does the CEO address the impatience inherent in young staff on a critical ESG issue they hold dear with the crushing responsibility of balancing revenue and shareholder considerations? The feedback channel to enable such two-way communications and conversations is fundamentally broken in large organizations. At the moment, when a staffer has a problem, either personal (low pay, over-work) or broadly about the company's operations (carbon footprint), the channels available to air griev-ances is limited in scope. Sure, on purely personal matters the staffer could go to his or her immediate supervisor and complain, which is a routine phenomenon. But there is no way for that supervisor to understand that such complaints have become rampant organization-wide and pose a serious risk to talent retention. This is because in the ongoing rush of conducting daily business, softer issues like talent management receive short shrift and company-wide platforms focus on weightier issues like boosting profits.

At the same time, the sure-fire response from most companies when staff complaints proliferate is to do an annual staff survey, which is a gargantuan bureaucratic exercise where the questions are massaged and nuanced so that the responses cause the least offense to Management (and also obscures serious underlying issues about the company's strategy and operations). It is no surprise that when something goes wrong in large companies, it is only a matter of time when disaffected staff, particularly millennials, decide to go public on their concerns. American tech major Google has learned this lesson through three high-profile public blowouts in as many years. The first kerfuffle concerned the company's decision to work with the Pentagon in developing artificial intelligence (AI) technology to analyze drone surveillance footage from the Department of Défense's vast operations targeting enemy combatants. Google staff reacted to Project Maven, as the project was known with fury and their agitation soon became public knowledge, forcing the company to retreat from supplying technology to the Pentagon. Similarly, Google faced staff pushback when it became known internally that the company was developing a search engine specifically tailored for China, which would presumably comply with the country's tough censorship and surveillance regulations. Over 1,400 Google staff signed on to an internal petition demanding that the company withdraw from the project. The petition promptly made its way to *The New York Times*, which reported[10] that employees had ques-tioned Google's apparent willingness to abide by China's

---

[10]Google Employees Protest Secret Work on Censored Search Engine for China – The New York Times, August 16, 2018.

censorship requirements, which "raised moral and ethnical issues." Google was soon forced to announce that it had no plans to expand into China. The final Google staff blowout came in 2021 when the company fired a well-respected artificial intelligence researcher Timnit Gebru over a research paper she had authored focused on technical aspects of an AI program on natural language processing which raised serious ethical and moral concerns.[11] According to media accounts, Gebru's superiors asked her to retract the paper or to modify it so that it was more acceptable to other departments who had raised concerns. When she apparently refused, Google fired Gebru, creating a media fire-storm about the company's commitment to protecting independence in research. The bigger lesson from multiple staff-related dramas which the American tech major has faced is that younger staff are deeply passionate about their work and blow the whistle, including to the media, when they feel that they are not being heard.

On a less dramatic scale, I observed this first-hand during a controversy surrounding the banking sector's support of palm oil plantations in South East Asia, a sector which was both a blessing (it transformed the agricultural fortunes of a handful of companies) and a curse (it lead to massive deforestation in Indonesia and displacement of wildlife). The typical reaction of millennial staff reading these facts will be to persuade/pressure the employer to withdraw completely from the palm oil sector. There are strong, compelling reasons for such a withdrawal – international bank support for palm oil plantations since the 1980s has helped create a small group of powerful conglomerates in Indonesia and Malaysia, who have wilfully and deliberately cleared vast swathes of rainforest in Borneo without safeguards and environmental protections. The Indonesian authorities until recently provided nominal oversight and there is evidence of collusion at the local level between the plantations and provincial leaders. The anxiety of millennial staff reached fever pitch when a prominent international NGO Greenpeace showed up outside the international bank headquarters and distributed pamphlets about the ongoing destruction of

---

[11] I will not go into the paper itself in detail. For those interested, read a detailed account in MIT Review, December 4, 2020 (We read the paper that forced Timnit Gebru out of Google). Here is what it says.

Borneo. The pitch had an emotional twist too because an NGO campaigner showed up with an inflatable *orangutan*, the adorable ape species native to Borneo, which has witnessed loss of habitat since the plantations took over and is danger of becoming extinct.

As can be expected, the NGO protest activity and the accompanying social media campaign raised a great deal of consternation among younger staff. The bank ultimately did the right thing by backing away from lending into palm oil (and subsequently fossil fuels), which reassured staff about the institution's commitment to doing the right thing. For me, the experience highlighted that large, complex organizations generally don't have the right tools to deal with internal dissent and dialogue and this problem gets magnified when it comes to dealing with social media savvy young staff. Corporate mantras about protecting shareholder value and maximizing profits has gone out of fashion. Worse, it does not resonate with staff. A dramatic example of this mismatch in language and expectations between the gerontocracy and youth comes from outside the private sector – when climate activist Great Thunberg addressed[12] the United Nations General Assembly (UNGA) in September 2019. Her short speech was preceded by the usual sleep-inducing prognostications from heads of state about the poor state of the world and why the international community should be doing a better job. From year to year, the speeches delivered by heads of state does not change much in tone and text. It is therefore no surprise that a cursory glance of the audience in the cavernous UNGA building will show hundreds of delegates catching up with sleep or chatting with colleagues. Thunberg's speech, in the presence of UN Secretary General Antonio Gutteres, woke everyone up because she started by saying the following: "My message is that we'll watching you. This is all wrong. I shouldn't be up here. I should be back in school on the other side of the ocean. Yet you all come to us young people for hope. How dare you?". There were more "how dare you" references as Thunberg went on to say something

---

[12]Transcript: Greta Thunberg's Speech at the UN Climate Action Summit – September 23, 2019. Source: National Public Radio.

which resonates with young people I meet. "You have stolen my dreams and my childhood with your empty words. And yet I'm one of the lucky ones. People are suffering. People are dying. Entire ecosystems are collapsing." *She added that "we" are in the beginning of mass extinction, and "all you can talk about" is money and fairy tales of eternal economic growth. "How dare you!".* (Italics mine)

Switching gears, I wonder what the reaction of a CEO would be if a young staff member addressed him or her in the same tone and anger which Thunberg expressed in her speech at the UN. Although corporate America and Europe has changed and become more tolerant of dissent and push-back, the over-whelming desire of the Human Resource department in such a case would be to censure the employee or to terminate employment. This will be taken as a savage indictment but in my experience, the HR department of large organizations are essentially dysfunctional and tone-deaf to staff concerns. I am no longer surprised that when a CEO is looking around to task someone with "change management," the task usually falls on the hapless HR chief who quickly assembles an internal team of HR experts who do as little internal consultation as possible. If Greta Thunberg were an Assistant VP or trainee at a large institution, instead of running a ruthlessly effective global campaign for climate change, she would probably be shown the door in a matter of weeks. For a global crisis as critical as climate change, you need multiple pressure points on the corporate sector, internal and external, to force companies to switch gears and to decarbonize at a significantly faster pace. Younger staff are superbly designed for this task because a majority of them get the science and are passionate about pro-tecting the planet. Their long-term incentives are aligned with the urgency to act because they, unlike the corporate gerontocracy currently in charge, will be around when the earth warms at an unsustainable pace and at the frontline of climate distress. What can then be done to remedy the power imbalance in large cor-porations where C-suite objectives are short-term and essentially focused on the here and now?

These issues go to the very heart of the modern organizational structure, which can date its provenance both to the modern army's general staff structure, which originated with the Prussian Army of the nineteenth century and management gurus Peter Drucker and Alfred P. Sloan's pioneering work in the 1930s and 1940s. Corporate generals love the Army's command and control structure for several reasons. First, it keeps them firmly in charge as they have oversight over major decisions or in many cases almost every decision taken by the company. Second, it instils a sense of discipline among the ranks because the effectiveness of command and control depends on everyone in the structure toeing the official line. Third, and this is regarded as a positive, it reinforces group think in the senior and junior ranks over a shared purpose. Finally, command and control works ineffectively when dissent is squashed and bad news sometimes takes a long time to filter up to the high command. Peter Drucker, who has written admiringly about the Prussian Army's innovations in structure was an enthusiastic champion of the Army's way of doing things, which he believed should be replicated by the corporate sector. "The master of management teaching Peter Drucker often turned to the military of his adopted nation," which was America, especially on matters of leadership, according to *Harvard Business Review*,[13] which quotes from the guru's 1967 book "The Effective Executive." In today's context, Drucker's advice makes for shocking reading. "It is the duty of the executive to remove ruthlessly anyone – who consistently fails to perform with high distinction," Drucker writes, "to let such a man stay on corrupts the others. It is grossly unfair to the whole organisation." He adds that it is also grossly unfair to the man's subordinates "who are deprived of their superior's inadequacy of opportunities for achievement and recognition." Finally, in a moment of compassion, Drucker says that it is "senseless cruelty" to the underperformer himself who "knows" he is inadequate "whether he admits to himself or not." Drucker was a hugely

[13]What Ever Happened to Accountability – Harvard Business Review, October 2012. Drucker's master thesis on the Prussian Army history and structure was published in winter 1941 (What became of the Prussian Army) and can be accessed, among many places, from the Virginia Quarterly Review (VQR).

influential management guru of his time and his thinking on organization structure and management incentives still permeates corporate thinking in America and to a lesser extent Europe. Alfred P. Sloan has also left a lasting imprint on thinking in corporate America with his original idea dating back to 1924, which segmented GM's brands based on price and customer preferences. The management guru industry has of course evolved since the Sloan and Drucker eras, with no shortage of new ideas and techniques to motivate and manage in the work place. Silicon Valley has made a major contribution by originating what on paper might appear to be bold and radical ideas on flattening organizational hierarchies and providing staff with the ability to innovate. The founder's myth remains strong in the Valley and building multi-billion corporations out of a garage reinforces the perception that these remain among the most progressive companies in the world. The sad aspect of Silicon Valley firms is that as they mature, they mimic the behaviors of the traditional large corporation and soon become consumed with internal bureaucratic disorder as we have witnessed with Meta and Google. In Europe, organizational structures are even more traditional and the legacy of the Prussian Army's general staff structure lives on.

A skeptic reading this chapter may challenge my presumption that the millennial generation's aspirations and work style are so different that organizations have to adapt and change. If profit maximization is the sole motive of the corporation, I would agree that the business case for change is weak. Placed in the wider ESG context, the millennial generation should be at the high table when major decisions are taken. Here the German model of "codetermination," which requires significant employee representation on the supervisory boards of large companies is a model. "Most German companies are content with this model because it leads to less internal conflict," says Sebastian Sick,[14] "They find it easier to fulfill management strategy once they know the employees are behind it." Why not have young people or youth advocacy groups on the main or advisory board of companies in

---

[14]Sebastian Sick is from the Hans Bockler Foundation, which advocates for codetermination rights. The quote is taken from an article in Insigniam – In Germany, a law to give employees a voice (and a vote).

America and the UK? This is likely to elicit groans from C-suites, where such an engagement structure will be regarded as a waste of time. However, for intergenerational equity and to ensure that companies don't take a detour from ESG goals, giving youth a voice on the future direction of the corporation is a moral imperative. This is one of the most important ways of making ESG great again, which we turn to in our final chapter.

9

MAKING ESG GREAT AGAIN

Better Metrics, Better Disclosure, Better Intentions Are the Path to ESG Nirvana.

Imagine we are in the year 2050, the precise period when the rich world was expected to achieve net zero in their emissions. Things have not gone as well as can be expected. When policymakers set these targets decades ago, there was an assumption that reality will eventually catch up with rhetoric, forcing countries and business to act. However, developed countries turned out to be in serious breach of their commitments and developing nations, unsurprisingly, followed the same approach. Meanwhile there has been a relentless rise in global warming with the UNFCCC predicting that global temperatures will exceed the 1.5 degree target set by a wide margin, perhaps to 2.5 or even 3 degrees. A significant portion of the planet is facing the full climactic wrath of rising ground temperatures, unprecedented flooding, droughts, and forest fires.

The rich have decamped to Scandinavia or New Zealand, the only habitable parts of the planet with warm winters and ever warmer summers. Two former CEOs, one American and the other European meet at a bar in Helsinki. It is January, warm and sweaty compared with Januarys past for over a millennia. There is no air-conditioning as persistent power shortages have knocked out energy systems.

Wistfully raising a glass of lukewarm beer, the American remarks:

The Scandinavians are different from us

The European responds:

Yes, they had better ESG metrics.

With deepest respects to Ernest Hemingway and F. Scott Fitzgerald[1] for paraphrasing their famous observation on the rich, I present this entirely fictional anecdote as a way of illustrating the stakes involved for the business community in grappling with climate change and in implementing what they have promised to do in their glossy annual reports. I also hope my valiant attempt at climate fiction[2] turns out to be fiction but the prospects for that unfortunately look gloomy. As we have discussed in the book, the global debate about climate action and all things ESG rests on the rather flawed premise that the business community will eventually do the right thing. If you aggregate all the ESG promises and the lofty commitments made by companies in recent years, there should have been tangible evidence of progress. The fact that the needle has barely moved, with promised actions back-loaded into the next few decades, is a sign that the entire ESG enterprise has been built on shaky foundations. How then, to use the title of this book, to make ESG less notorious, and to use the title of this chapter, to make it great again?

The ESG complex is being buffeted by two forces – centripetal and centrifugal – which is imploding as we speak. This is an engineering impossibility but perfectly illustrates the dilemma at hand. Centripetal forces are aligning the business community with a set of global norms, regulations, and standards. The keyword here is convergence. The centrifugal force, which is pulling it apart, is due to sharp divergences in practice and even sharper disagreements on

---

[1]The full quote is set out below and never happened in an actual conversation: Fitzgerald: "The rich are different from us." Hemingway: "Yes, they have more money."
[2]For those interested, two of the best works of climate fiction are The Ministry of Future (by Kim Stanley Robinson) and Gun Island (by Amitav Ghosh).

definitional issues, which partially explains the furore over greenwashing.

This confusion has empowered critics on the right to dismiss ESG as "woke capitalism" and for seemingly sensible voices like *The Economist* to proclaim that narrowing and simplifying ESG metrics is perhaps the way to go. The choice here – between abolishing ESG altogether or dumbing it down – betrays a fundamental lack of understanding as to why environmental, social, governance has become such a powerful and controversial issue. Stripping it down to the basics, I believe that a company with a strong record of ESG compliance is a proof point of how a modern corporation is supposed to function in the second decade of the twenty-first century. We could disagree over the social purpose of a corporation or the metrics to evidence that, but it is impossible to fathom a return to the Friedman ethos of maximizing shareholder value and profits. So like it or not ESG is here to stay and we have to figure out the best possible way of making it work.

At the heart of the controversy surrounding ESG is a design flaw. In attempting to be the catch-all phrase to describe the activities of a socially committed company, a significant amount of content is lost in translation. To grossly simplify the tension, here is how different stakeholders view the promise and potential of ESG:

P1. Climate activists see ESG as a powerful way for companies to respond to climate change.

P2. Investors want certainty that the companies they are investing in have world-class governance, treat employees and suppliers fairly, and have tangible net zero targets.

P3. International NGOs want a radical change in corporate behaviors by, for example, requiring a complete withdrawal from fossil fuels and for significant improvement in social impact.

P4. Financial markets see ESG as a new asset class where investors can trade in stocks, bonds, and other instruments based on better disclosure and comparative ESG performance.

P5. National governments and regulators are struggling to reconcile upcoming global ESG standards with the stark reality of the local business community simply not being prepared for the change in purpose, culture, and metrics which investors are demanding.

Given the conflicting priorities of the various stakeholders, it is no wonder that we are in ESG hell. Let's focus on *P2* and *P4* since we have covered the others in detail elsewhere in the book. Stuart Kirk, the same gentleman we met in an earlier chapter and who had to leave HSBC Asset Management for making intemperate remarks about "some nut job" telling him "about the end of the world," has actually come up with sensible suggestions to improve ESG's standing in financial markets. Writing in *Financial Times*,[3] Kirk argues that ESG has an "existential defect" which needs fixing, very much the same point I make above. "The flaw is that ESG has carried two meanings from birth" he writes "Regulators have never bothered disentangling them, so the whole industry speaks and behaves at cross purposes." Kirk says that "one meaning" is how portfolio managers, analysts, and data companies have understood ESG investing for years. "That is: 'taking' environmental, social, and governance issues into account when trying to assess the potential risk-adjusted returns of an asset. Most funds are ESG on this basis."

This expansive investing approach defined by Kirk pre-supposes that investors are aware that they are putting money into companies with superior ESG frameworks and metrics, not perfect or absolute by any means. As Kirk argues, this is very different from the second category of ESG investing in "ethical" or "green" or "sustainable assets." This second meaning, he says, is how most people think of ESG – trying to do the right thing with their money. "They prefer a company that doesn't burn coal, eschews nepotism, and has diverse senior executives. This conflict leads to myriad misunderstandings." In Kirk's definition, the first category of investments would fall under "ESG-inputs," where ESG risks, however material, are considered less important than "other drivers" of returns. The second category, defined as "ESG-output" funds would only invest in sustainable assets which meets *all* categories of environmental, social, governance goals which an institutional investor requires. For example, ESG-output fund managers would take an absolutist and purist approach in selecting fully

---

[3]ESG is existentially flawed and must be split into two – Stuart Kirk, Financial Times, September 2, 2022.

ESG-compliant stocks to invest in, based on available comparative data. While Kirk has constructed a useful methodology to consider the differences in ESG investing approaches, it still begs the question, three to be precise, on what investors seem desperate to get an answer to:

How can we be sure about the comparability of ESG data i.e. are we comparing apples with apples or apples with various other fruits?

With all of the attention on ESG as an investing class, it should deliver superior financial returns compared with companies which are not fully compliant (ESG-input funds, under Kirk's definition).

How do we prevent companies from massaging their ESG data to present a false and misleading picture of their actual performance?

All of these questions and the tensions underlying them unraveled in a spectacular fashion at Deutsche Asset Management (DWS), the fund management arm of banking giant Deutsche Bank. The case involves a whistle-blower, Desiree Fixler, who was appointed Chief Sustainability Officer of DWS in 2020 and exited less than a year later after making high-profile allegations that DWS was greenwashing its ESG investment credentials and reporting. Full disclosure – I know Ms. Fixler and have met with her twice in my previous role at the international bank. However, I have not spoken to her about the case and the material below was pieced together using publicly available information. It is no exaggeration to say that Ms. Fixler's complaint about DWS practices represents the most prominent case of greenwashing and has shaken and stirred the asset management industry to focus on better metrics and compliance. The substance of the whistle-blower's allegations is as follows, with an account first from Morningstar.[4] Fixler was hired to advance the firm's ESG efforts, but says she quickly encountered resistance. Specifically, it was the 2020 annual report that became a bone of contention. According to Fixler, the board insisted on

---

[4]DWS and the global crackdown on greenwashing – Morningstar, September 19, 2022.

reporting 459 billion euros in assets-under-management as "ESG-integrated" in the annual report" according to Morningstar.

Under the EU's Sustainable Finance Disclosures Regulation (SFDR), there are clear guidelines on what investments could be classified as truly sustainable (and what investments take ESG factors into account but are not fully sustainable). Ms. Fixler alleged that the number provided by DWS was "inflated many times over," providing a misleading picture of the asset manager's true exposure to purely sustainable investments. To get really technical, here is the full extract from the Morningstar report: "Fixler says DWS used what it calls the 'ESG Engine', a tool fed with data and scores from MSCI, ISS, Morningstar Sustainanalytics that combined information on thousands of companies. Using weighted averages, the score was calculated." The end result, according to Fuxler, was made available to DWS' portfolio managers and "was enough for the board to apply the label 'ESG-integrated' to products in its prospectuses."

The reader may well get bored with the technical description cited above and ask "so what"? Ms. Fixler's allegations go to the heart of how investment funds label their portfolios as being green or ESG compliant. Billions, if not trillions of dollars in pension funds and long-term capital are ready to be deployed based on ESG considerations provided by an asset manager and if they get it wrong (or are wilfully manipulating the data as the DWS case allegedly illustrates) there is a huge risk that greenwashing is for real, damaging the entire sector. We have heard Ms. Fixler's point of view and to provide a sense of balance, it is useful to hear the DWS position.

DWS has fiercely rejected Ms. Fixler's claims that she was wrongfully dismissed after her whistle-blower complaint, a claim that was upheld in a German court in January 2022. Things get even more intriguing from here on with German police raiding DWS offices and parent Deutsche Bank on May 31, 2022 on suspicion of capital investment fraud. Senior German public prosecutor had this to say[5] about what prompted the authorities to raid DWS. "After an examination sufficient evidence has emerged" that, contrary to the

---

[5]German officials raid Deutsche Bank's DWS over "greenwashing claims" – Reuters, May 31, 2022.

information in the sales prospectuses of DWS funds, ESG criteria were actually only taken in a minority of investments "but were not taken into account in a large number of investments." This was potentially labeled as prospectus fraud under German law and the police raid had immediate ramifications on DWS. CEO Asoka Woehrmann departed the firm in June 2022, the first and possibly the highest profile corporate leader to resign over allegations of greenwashing.

Let these words sink in – the first and possibly the highest profile corporate leader to resign over allegations of greenwashing. DWS still faces penalties if the German courts find that they violated securities laws and we should suspend judgment until the case is resolved. Some historical perspective is helpful here. During the height of the global financial crisis in 2008, plenty of American and European bankers lost their jobs because of financial mismanagement on a grand scale but none were dragged to the courts for either misleading investors about the full extent of the firm's financial troubles or for failing to act decisively to address the meltdown. Ultimately, it was the taxpayers who came through by bailing out these august financial institutions. The German case against DWS is not due to the firm creating a systemic financial crisis but the underlying principle is an important one – even in a topic as arcane as ESG, institutions better be careful about how they are labeling their financial products and marketing them with supposed ESG benefits. Woehrmann himself was defiant in his communications to staff on his exit. "The allegations made against DWS and me over the past months, including personal attacks and threats, however unfounded and undefendable have left a mark," Woehrmann said in an email to staff,[6] "They have been a burden for the firm, as well as for me, most significantly, for those closest to me."

Woehrmann's woes might seem to be a specifically European case but regulators in the UK and America are likely to follow the DWS case closely to establish if they should follow the same rule-book. "Increased regulatory scrutiny and enforcement in this market is changing behavior," investment firm Jeffries noted in a

---

[6]DWS CEO exit is helpful deterrent for greenwashing – Reuters, June 1, 2022.

report. This followed a suit filed in a German court by a consumer group against DWS "for allegedly misrepresenting an investment fund's green credentials in marketing materials."[7] In a statement provided to *Reuters*, DWS noted the following: "We have examined the documents in focus in detail and remain convinced that the DWS advertising communications – comply with legal requirements." The case is ongoing and consumer groups will be actively monitoring the legal outcome to establish if there are grounds to take legal action against other institutions making similar tall claims in their advertising. We have seen in earlier chapters the tendency of large corporations to puff up their sustainability rhetoric in annual reports and how, in many cases, it has little or no connection with the actual performance. Well, the DWS action provides an opening to investor and consumer groups to closely examine truth-telling in ESG reports and advertising and to pursue legal claims if they believe that the claims fall short.

While institution's may well tone down their advertising and ESG promotion, this still leaves open the wide question on the role of credit rating agencies and information aggregators in properly labeling ESG funds in the marketplace. If the allegations against DWS' mislabeling their funds as ESG-integrated holds up in the German court,[8] there is an immense task for rating agencies and information providers. I say this with a degree of skepticism – credit rating agencies did not cover themselves in glory during the global financial crisis by providing flawed, positive scores for mortgage-backed securities that eventually crashed the system. The regulatory noose has tightened in the aftermath of 2008 but as was the case before, the business model of the troika dominating the space (S&P, Moody's, Fitch) remains unchanged. They still get paid by the companies they are rating, which creates a perverse incentive structure. "Even assuming the intent of inappropriate behaviour, attempting to systematically let commercial interest dilute analytical

---

[7] Both the quote from Jeffries and the details of the case brought by the consumer group are from Banking Dive – Deutsche Bank's DWS sued over "confusing" ESG claim – October 24, 2022.
[8] According to reports, DWS settled the case filed by the consumer watch-dog in March 2023. It agreed to a "cease and desist" declaration, refraining from marketing certain features of one of its funds.

independence would put the lucrative business model at grave risk," warned a 2021 paper[9] from the UN's Department of Economic and Social Affairs (DESA). The paper's primary focus was on perceived biases in the way rating agencies approaches sovereign default risk between advanced and emerging economies. As we will discuss shortly, there is no agreed methodology in analyzing and understanding ESG risks in emerging and developing countries, which has the potential for rating agencies over-stating the risk factors compared with similar issues in developed countries.

As it happens, even in Europe, the European securities regulator ESMA found[10] a high level of divergence in disclosure of ESG factors in credit ratings. ESMA's research narrowed on 64,000 press releases issues by credit rating agencies in the 2019–2020 period on ESG matters, based on specific regulatory guidelines issued by ESMA in early 2020. Using natural language processing techniques to mine ESG-specific mentions in the press releases issued by credit rating agencies, ESMA's broad conclusion was that the level of disclosure differed significantly and there were divergences "even for rated entities that are highly exposed to ESG factors." While agreeing that the rating agencies may deploy different methodological processes to assess ESG risks, the ESMA findings made it clear that disclosure practices varied between them. "It is unclear why some CRAs (credit rating agencies) deem ESG factors to be relevant and report them in their press releases, while others do not yet do so – especially in the case of credit rating agencies for issuers who are classified as highly ESG-exposed according to public data or according to other CRAs rating these same issuers or their instruments. The divergences we find across CRAs in this respect are, therefore, quite striking."

Translating ESMA's findings into plain English can be best done through a hypothetical example. It must be under-scored that the primary objective of a credit rating agency is to apply a rating on the credit worthiness of a company i.e. are the company's business and financial prospects sound and stable? ESG considerations add a

---

[9]Credit rating agencies and developing economies – UN DESA Working Paper, December 2021.
[10]Text mining ESG disclosures in rating agency press releases – European Securities and Markets Authority, February 10, 2022.

layer of complexity as I will illustrate. AAA is a power utility company in Germany which generates energy from fossil fuels, coal and natural gas. AAA is what the media used to describe as a "blue-chip" company in the old days because of its consistent track record in delivering stable revenues and profits. However, the company's exposure to coal makes its environmental disclosures highly relevant from an ESG perspective, while its natural gas dependence potentially provides it with a lift because of its (controversial) role as a bridge fuel.

Suppose the credit rating agencies providing a rating for AAA's issuance of equity or bonds take divergent approaches – CRA 1 focuses on natural gas and the company's promise to increase the fuel as a share of its feedstock. CRA 1 is impressed with the direction of travel, financial prospects, and issues a favorable ESG rating. On the other hand, analysts at CRA 11 are far from impressed by AAA's continued dependence on coal and issue a damaging ESG rating. How to explain the sharp differences in approach? CRA1 is likely to argue that what mattered most (in the ratings decision) was is the company's promised reshaping of its feedstock mix toward natural gas. CRA11 on the other hand is focused on the here and now and believes that AAAs reliance on coal was a major negative and therefore applied the negative rating. I am grossly over-simplifying the ratings process here of course. Meanwhile a pension fund investor in Canada is a long-term investor in AAA and has enjoyed steady dividend inflows over the past decade. The pension fund is under pressure from the teacher's union (whose money it is managing) to exit from fossil fuels altogether from the portfolio. Using CRA1's rating formulation, the pension fund could either stay invested in AAA on the promise of an exit from coal or rely on CRA11 which believes that the utility is heavily exposed to fossil fuels and deserved a negative rating. In the real world, it must be said that a teacher's union would include natural gas in its definition of fossil fuels and require the pension fund to withdraw from AAA altogether. At its core, investor decisions to stay invested in companies like AAA and to apply and explain the favorable CRA1 ESG label on its portfolio is greenwashing in summary. How to mitigate this and build greater credibility in the analysis and insights provided by credit rating agencies?

The credit rating agencies talk a good talk when it comes to explaining and defending their ESG ratings approaches. Here is S & P on[11] its S & P Global ESG Scores. "Unlike ESG datasets that reply simply on publicly available information, S & P Global ESG Scores are uniquely informed by a combination of verified company disclosures, media and stakeholder analysis, and in-depth company engagement via the S & P Global Corporate Sustainability Assessment (CSA), providing unparalleled access to ESG insights before they reach others." If this isn't enough in terms of hyperbole, S & P adds that its approach "form the basis of a unique ecosystem that actively drives corporate disclosures and raises the bar on sustainability standards over time." Moody's performs slightly better by explaining the methodology behind its ratings process, for example on how ESG considerations are integrated into credit analysis.[12] "Moody's credit analysis seeks to incorporate all issues that can materially impact credit quality, including ESG and climate risk: and aims to take the most forward-looking perspective that visibility into these risks and mitigants permits." Now both S&P, Moody's and Fitch, the third agency which completes the global ratings troika are dominant players and have the power and the influence to reshape investor decisions on ESG issues. Thus, despite greater regulatory and investor attention in the aftermath of the global financial crisis, they are clearly stumbling in this space.

Making ESG great again will require many things but improving the credit rating process is an integral part of the overall solution. To ensure that I am not attributing all of the troubles in the ESG space down to poor credit rating credibility, let's once again return to large corporate institutions – banks, tech companies, manufacturers – who play a dominant role in shaping ESG outcomes. We have spent a considerable amount of time in this book exploring ESG issues in advanced countries, mainly Europe and America. But the rubber really hits the road in regions where ESG ideas, practice, and implementation is lagging behind – the emerging and developing world. My ESG work has straddled the developed and

---

[11]S & P Global ESG scores – from company website www.spglobal.com.
[12]Moody's ESG – Four components to MIS integration of ESG – from www.esg.moodys.io.

developing world and the challenges and the greenwashing opportunities are immense. Exploring these issues is deserving of a separate book, which I hope someone will tackle in the future. For the moment, let's explore three tensions in moving toward better ESG understanding in the developing world:

First, developing countries are far behind in articulating climate approaches and in setting net zero targets. This has resulted in many countries believing that targets could be postponed well into the future. There are exceptions of course (China, India come to mind) but a majority of the developing world is struggling to deal with a warming planet.

Second, even if there is good intention in implementing better social outcomes, the legal and legislative frameworks in many developing countries are creaky and out-of-date. Compliance with global standards tend to be in sectors which are outwardly focused on exports. Building capacity from the ground up takes time and effort.

Finally, multinational corporations have taken on the responsibility of imposing ESG conditions and better compliance on companies they do business with in the developing world. An international bank, as discussed earlier in the book, can hold up financing for a textile or shoe wear client if there are allegations about worker abuse or environmental neglect. While MNCs play an important role in transferring global knowledge and know-how in the countries they operate in, their own ESG record has been decidedly patchy.

This raises the immediate question on the accuracy of ESG ratings provided by the global troika in cases where the MNC sources a significant amount of production in the developing world. There is greater NGO scrutiny of course since the infamous Nike case of the early 1990s which serves as a natural check against potential abuses. But accessing the right data and integrating it into a comparable and understandable global ESG model is still out of reach. This factor alone seriously disadvantages companies from the emerging and developing world, who are keen to access capital from global markets, comply with best ESG practice, but still face barriers. There are nascent efforts, including from the Glasgow

Financial Alliance for Net Zero (GFANZ) to help build the needed framework to mobilize capital but this is a multiyear effort.

Jacques Attali, a former French policymaker builds a persuasive case[13] when he argues that "the reality of emerging countries and their industries" in any global ESG framework or model "must" be urgently brought to the fore. "The current ESG system remains an artifact from advanced economies, generally favouring companies from these same economies. Capturing 90% of related financial flows, they leave an astonishingly marginal space for emerging markets' companies, with the remaining 10% being still unevenly distributed among a handful of fast-growing Asian economies." He adds that the root of the polarization lies in the lack of "shared standards and analytical frameworks" to measure ESG commitment. Standardization initiatives are either individual, through the development of "non-reproducible, specific, and opaque methods" designed by sovereign issuers or carried out by private or nongovernmental actors, which generally leave behind emerging markets' companies. "Indeed, major rating agencies remain mostly located in and primarily focused on developed markets, causing them to blindly apply the same standards to all companies they are allegedly rating, inevitably incorporating cultural and geographical biases in ESG scores."

Global investors like private equity funds acutely feel this disconnect because they would like to increase their investible capital into emerging and developing countries but poor ESG measurement tools and disclosure is holding many of them back. As we discussed in the hypothetical AAA case, investors into these PE funds are also becoming picky and want to stay away from companies where the ESG articulation is unclear. As things stand, the large rating agencies and data providers in the sustainability space offer only cursory coverage of companies from emerging markets or the developing world. There is coverage of a few "trophy" companies in this space, as I have discovered, but nothing which rises up to the category of a distinct emerging markets ESG asset class. Trickle down approaches built on the belief that global standards

---

[13]Current ESG scheme leaves emerging economies' efforts unrewarded – By Jacques Attali, Nikkei Asia, March 9, 2022.

will simply cascade down to developing countries through loan conditions or tougher compliance are not working. A fundamental reset in thinking is required.

What would be the grand plan to prevent greenwashing and to make ESG data comparable and meaningful across the developed and developing world? I believe that the ESG space has suffered serious reputation damage and headwinds, in the form of political pressure and greater investor skepticism, are only likely to increase in intensity. Calls for urgently reforming or streamlining ESG disclosure and data implies that time is running out to rebuild credibility. Incremental reforms and fixes, which have become the norm, will aggravate rather than address the problem. What I have in mind are four reforms, which will form the basis of an ESG manifesto, which will reshape ESG into a cohesive, explainable, comparative, and impactful asset class, with significant collateral positive impact of saving the planet.

Cohesion first. Quite simply, the ESG enterprise is over-burdened and overwhelmed with a multiplicity of global, regional, public, and private efforts. Some of these efforts are genuinely designed for progress (TCFD, for example), while there are many others (particularly on the private sector side) which are virtue signaling efforts that allows companies to communicate that they are on the side of the angels and in extremely good company. The utility of some well-meaning private sector initiatives must also be questioned. There is a Taskforce for Nature Markets, independent of the Science Based Targets Initiative. Should they be merged? Proponents of both will furiously note that the initiatives have clearly defined objectives, have secured private sector buy-in, and also engage with regulators. My point is that all of them add to the clutter in the ESG space, confusing investors and the public at large. Cohesion will require aggregation and consolidation of all things ESG, not just the environment pillar which is the norm, and no one is better placed to play this role as financial and securities regulators.

Singapore's central bank, the Monetary Authority of Singapore (MAS) has been progressive by building such a cohesive approach. On one level, the central bank's guidelines are mainly focused on environmental management issues – with TCFD implementation at the core, requiring all listed companies on the Singapore Exchange to provide climate reporting on a "comply or explain" basis. This has immediately expanded the scope of climate reporting from beyond the financial sector, which the central bank has jurisdiction over. One level below, the MAS has also moved to strengthen disclosure and reporting guidelines for retail ESG funds, as a way to mitigate the risk of greenwashing. "The guidelines will facilitate greater comparability in the disclosures made by retail ESG funds, which in turn will allow more informed investment decisions," the MAS guidelines note.[14] European regulators have also taken the global lead in developing a sustainable finance taxonomy but the entire project has been mired in controversy and confusion. The MAS' streamlined approach, which included significant consultation with the private sector, has raised investor awareness and built guardrails on what is acceptable from an ESG investment perspective.

Greater cohesion will help in better explainability and standardization of ESG approaches and metrics. At the moment, to put this politely, this space is a mess with listed companies defining their own ESG approaches and key performance indicators (KPIs). The sustainability reports of two companies in the same industry and geography differs sharply in scope and metrics. How can we foster some level of standardization, as the TCFD has done with climate disclosures or the streamlined energy and carbon reporting (SECR) guidelines? In supply chain management or in diversity and inclusion, companies use their own peculiar set of metrics. The UK has taken the lead here in two significant areas. On gender diversity, rules now require that employers with 250 or more staff should report and publish their gender pay gap information in a uniform template. Similarly, on preventing abuse in supply chains, UK companies are required under the Modern Slavery Act to report and confirm at Board level each year that modern slavery practices do not exist in their supply chains. There are penalties for failing to disclose or breaches in the rules, which sent a collective chill down the spine of UK Boards who did not devote adequate time and resources to examine their company's supply chain management.

---

[14]Monetary Authority of Singapore – Disclosure and Reporting Guidelines for Retail ESG funds, July 28, 2022.

The UK rules overall enable companies to explain three important components of their ESG offering (climate, diversity, supply chains). A similar regulatory effort will be an uphill battle across the pond due to corporate lobbying and fragmentation of rules and supervisors. The golden mean for investors in the ESG space is comparability of data across industry sectors and borders. If the data and the rules of the road are not comparable, it creates perverse arbitrage opportunities for investors. The World Economic Forum estimates[15] that there are more than 600 ESG ratings and rankings in use today, "creating an overwhelming data challenge" for investors and businesses. Multiple ESG ratings allow companies to "cherry pick" the most flattering providers in a practice known as greenwashing. Comparing corporate progress across so many metrics is all but impossible. Standardizing ESG data should be the responsibility of regulators, with input from the rating agencies and the private sector. Building a global ESG data standard may be an impossible objective but the future credibility and integrity of the asset class will depend on how much standardization (or harmonization) can be achieved.

The last pillar of my ESG manifesto is impact, not just for ESG as an asset class but ESG for greater societal impact. In the rush to dissect the merits and challenges of ESG, it is tempting to forget what is at stake. I was reminded of this when I holidayed in an idyllic part of the vast Northern Californian coast-line last year. The location was Sea Ranch, a utopian community in northern Sonoma County. You are not alone during a morning walk on the rugged, uneven, and spectacular ocean front. Lazing on the jagged rocks each morning was a family of Harbour seals and pups – for all we know with not a worry in the world as they feasted on the ocean's rich harvest of protein. The seals may instinctively understand that the climate is changing and the decimation of much of the treasured redwood forests in this part of California are silent testimony to that damage and destruction. California is privileged and prosperous and better positioned to handle all that Mother

---

[15]Here's why comparable ESG reporting is crucial for investors – World Economic Forum, July 8, 2021.

Nature may throw at this land. The developing world and a majority of the population are not so fortunate. Fundamentally, getting ESG right is not just to improve investor returns or to bolster the credibility of the CEO class. As philosopher William Macaskill warns in *Foreign Affairs*[16] the fossil record indicates that the average mammal species lasts a million years. By this measure alone we have about 700,000 years ahead of us. "The fact that humanity is only in its infancy highlights what a tragedy its untimely death would be," he writes. Let me break this down in the language of corporate gurus. Should business wish to fulfill its core social purpose this century, it must recognize that E, S, and G should be both the A, B, and C of how they do business and the X, Y, and Z in shaping positive outcomes for people and the planet. If they fall short, humanity will pay the ultimate price.

---

[16]The Beginning of History – Surviving The Era of Catastrophic Risk – William Macaskill, Foreign Affairs, September–October 2022.

EPILOGUE – THE INTERVIEWS

Now that you have read what I have to say about ESG and the role of business, I thought it would be useful to test the hypothesis of the book with a few experts. I deliberately decided not to interview current CEOs or corporate executives for two reasons. First, the internal process for securing approval for the final text would be formidable. Second, even after navigating the afore-mentioned process, it is questionable if the companies would have something interesting to say. Being a former corporate propagandist myself, I can assert with some confidence that companies cannot resist the temptation of staying on propaganda on a contentious issue like ESG. All of this makes me a cynical person I know, but I decided that the best option would be to interview people who once served in senior roles in corporations and are now somewhat removed. In terms of process, none of the interviewees reviewed the manuscript before the interviews, enabling them to speak freely about the issues.

Vasuki Shastry

V. SHANKAR

I first met V. Shankar in Bombay in 1985, when I was a pesky journalist for a business magazine, and he was a rising investment banker. He is a Cofounder and Chief Executive Officer of Gateway Partners, an emerging markets-centered private equity fund domiciled in Singapore and Dubai. Prior to Gateway, Shankar was CEO – Middle East, Africa, Europe, and the Americas, and a member of the global board of Standard Chartered Bank Plc and held senior roles in America and Asia at the Bank of America. In the spirit of full disclosure, I am an ESG Advisor for Gateway Partners.

Q. As a manager of an emerging markets-centered private equity fund, how relevant and realistic are the evolving global ESG standards in your investment footprint?

A. First thing I would like to say that we are all starting off, to use golfing analogy, with different handicaps. Developed markets are like Tiger Woods and developing countries are amateurs. Their fiscal and financial capacity is substantially different so taking a one-size-fits-all approach is a problem. Is this a global problem that we all need to resolve and converge? The answer is a resounding yes. The question is the pace. If you look at the previous commitments made by the west to support emerging markets come up to speed, more than 80% of the commitments by some calculations have not been met. Emerging markets need help, albeit emerging markets are a vast swathe of territory. Some of them, China, and India for example, are well equipped to handle this financially. On the other extreme, you have poor African countries like Burkina Faso and its peers who lack the financial, operating, and technical capacity. They need support and whatever commitments will be made this time around can't just be bark and all talk, they need to be tangible and have a bite.

Q. How do you ensure this?

One possible way of ensuring commitments have bite is for countries being able to pledge IMF-issued SDRs (special drawing rights) as collateral so that the funding is available through a multilateral institution like the IMF or World Bank rather than relying on the good graces of governments which often change in democracies. We have seen commitments made by one administration reneged by another coming into power for whatever reason. Overall, emerging markets need time to fully comply with global ESG standards. My suggestion would be for a system akin to "handicapping" in golf where countries which are further along the journey should not go for net zero by 2050 but should probably do so by 2035 or 2040. Those countries which are substantially behind should have the climate space until 2060. So hypothetically, the whole world gets to net zero by that extended period. Developing countries need the financial and policy support. The other challenge is how we are measuring this. This is not refined mathematics where one plus one equals two. We can make these metrics so complex that we will all drown in it and merely stuff the pocket of consultants. By making it complex, we also make sure that the dice is loaded in favor of the larger firms. This is because they alone have the capacity, financial or technical, to measure and to report. Let's not make perfection the enemy of the good.

Q. You mentioned an extended period of net zero compliance for emerging and developing markets? What are some of the immediate challenges they face in getting started?

A. We need to fundamentally understand that there are trade-offs which represent the broader challenge you are alluding to. There are trade-offs between the creation of jobs and the environment, between governance and the social implications. You can see these trade-offs being discussed even in advanced markets like the United States. We need to also recognize that who sets the standards is an issue. For instance, on governance, we have somehow implicitly accepted that the western, Anglo-Saxon governance model is the best. That has not necessarily proven to be any better than many other forms of governance. Western boards are still stuffed with male, pale, and stale people. There have been flaws exposed in developed markets, as much rigging of the markets there as anywhere else. So how we go about setting standards and making sure all voices are included is important.

Q. As an asset manager complying with global standards, are you able to shape and influence the behaviors of the firms you invest in?

A. The answer to "are we able to influence" is yes. But implicit in that answer is that you don't want to be pushing water uphill. You want to invest in companies and managements that fundamentally believe in ESG and being a good corporate citizen. You cannot be selling fire insurance to an arsonist. Our philosophy is to invest in companies and managements that are committed to being a good corporate citizen and believe that by improving their "E", improving their "S", and improving their "G", they will benefit. There are also several good reasons why this approach is good. First, the DNA of the promoters of the business is an important investment consideration. Second, you don't want to be investing in something which will become a stranded asset. It could become stranded because it is going to be disrupted by a green-tech firm or somebody who is a better corporate citizen. You could get stranded because of changing consumer preference because of regulation. So, for all the reasons cited above, it is both a defense and offense strategy to incorporate ESG into your capital risk. However, let's not get carried away by extreme voices on either side of the debate. There is a role for moderate voices and for taking a calibrated approach because one size will not fit all.

Q. What would be an example of such a calibrated approach?

One good example is cement. One could argue that if cement were a country, it would be the third or fourth largest polluter in the world and therefore you should cease all production. But cement is a fundamental pillar of development. Should we say that Africans should not have cement and live in thatched huts. Or should we only use green cement which is going to cost multiple times as much as the traditional product? The answer is Africans need access to as much cement as they need because they are only now starting off on their development journey. This is to balance and nuance the issue between job security, food, development, and simultaneously tackle climate change.

Q. In your investment footprint of Africa, the Middle East, and South and Southeast Asia, there is a mix of developing and developed markets. Are there regional variations and can companies learn from each other in implementing better ESG standards?

A. This may not be music to everyone's ears. Al Gore became a missionary to promote climate change. But without China we would not be having the affordability in terms of solar or wind power which we are all enjoying today and has become a real alternative to fossil fuels. We can also talk endlessly about electric vehicles, but you must consider that two-thirds of EVs made today are in China. China seized this opportunity and is way ahead of the curve, and other emerging markets can learn from them. A quick follow-up is India, which was initially resisting the climate change debate and I have been in meetings where they said that we have coal and that is the cheapest form of energy. Now that the cost curve has changed, where solar can be produced almost at parity, India has become a big convert. It also becomes a business opportunity if you do it at scale. So, no we don't need to look at this just as a challenge. Then countries like Singapore and UAE come to mind which are further along the journey. So, the upshot is we don't need to necessarily learn from the United States or Europe.

Q. So as a corollary, the sustainable finance opportunity world-wide is so significant, are we getting preoccupied with achieving net zero targets?

A. It's a journey. We should have milestones along the way in terms of how we are progressing toward the goal. Reducing emissions by 50% is as effective as someone launching a new venture where the emissions footprint starts off at that level. That is the equation we need to work. So, coming back to cement, if we can find a way of reducing emissions by process improvements or alternative fuels, that is as good as or even better than building a new plant with 50% less emissions.

Q. As a former banker and current asset manager, do you see sustainable finance flourishing in the next five years in emerging markets?

A. Yes, finance can flourish but it is a follower. What creates the need for sustainable finance is a green project. You want demand to be created and there will be more green projects because of regulatory and societal pressures. The cost curve for green solutions also achieving parity with traditional fuels is also an important part of this equation. Which is why I believe that despite a lot of talk about hydrogen as a viable fuel or that of solid-state batteries, their commercial viability is not tested yet absent huge government subsidies. These will require time and investments in scale and technology, just as it took solar to achieve viability. Governments can indeed influence scale and adoption. Not just through subsidies but also through "industrial policy" which is anathema for die-hard believers in free markets! What President Biden has done through the Inflation Reduction Act (IRA) is effectively a new form of industrial policy at work. The last thing I would say is that we need to battle against our approach being hijacked by extreme voices. We also need to shut down "energy hypocrisy." It is ok for Europe to use coal but not ok for some emerging markets. It is ok for the United Kingdom to have gas and oil pipelines, but if Africa is doing it in Uganda or Tanzania, it is a problem and financing is not being made available. These are sheer double standards and hypocrisy.

DENIZ HARUT

Deniz Harut was my colleague at Standard Chartered Bank, where her primary focus areas were sovereign advisory and sustainable finance. She is currently an Executive Director of Pollination, the London-based specialist climate change investment and advisory firm. As the interview will demonstrate, Deniz is a thought leader in sustainable finance and has broad expertise in emerging markets, development finance, and in advising companies on net zero strategies and in navigating the climate transition.

Q. How do you concretely assess net zero plans of major financial institutions and the related concerns over companies postponing difficult decisions?

A. The direction of travel is clear, and the private sector has been quite decisive. Financial institutions (and markets) are reengineering their business models and integrating climate considerations and the broad potential impact. The drivers are two-fold. In the United Kingdom and the EU, it is the regulators who are providing the advanced push. Simultaneously, pressure has also built up from asset owners and institutional investors. We are also seeing shareholder activism on the rise and are observing more management teams being challenged on climate inaction. It has been a top-down process and understandably there will be leaders and there will be laggards.

Q. You mentioned that the push for greater disclosure is coming from financial regulators. How is this impacting the financial sector in terms of how they are preparing themselves for greater compliance?

A. The Taskforce for Climate Related Disclosures (TCFD) has become mandatory in many advanced jurisdictions. This has created a rush among financial institutions to get the right data and to address any immediate gaps or weaknesses. There are two elements to this challenge. First, banks and asset managers want to ensure that they are across the line when it comes to full compliance with the regulations. Second, some institutions are using this opportunity to completely reengineer their business models. They want to go beyond integrated reporting and figure out how they can thrive in a global economy which is decarbonizing, including the adaptation of new technologies. I am also seeing this in private markets and what is accelerating the process is the availability of shadow ratings on how a company is performing in terms of climate and nature impacts. At the end of the day, there will be winners (alpha) and there will be many others who will remain stagnant. I am encouraged that companies are taking a holistic approach and no longer looking at the climate challenge through the narrow lens of data management or risk approaches.

Q. You mentioned adaptation of new technologies in the climate and green space. Is that having a tangible, positive impact in accelerating the climate transition?

A. Most certainly, yes. There is a huge pipeline of venture capital in the climate-tech space which is becoming more visible and impactful. The most impressive aspect is it is taking place across the board and markets are also taking a view on pricing. The critical challenge is in building the adaptive capacity to facilitate the transition. So, you have entirely new ventures in carbon markets, in capturing carbon data and you are likely to see the emergence of many unicorns in this space.

Q. This is all encouraging but what about the capacity of C-suites and Boards? Are they well prepared to embrace the challenge and steer their companies on to the green transition?

A. There needs to be a shake-up. The fundamental challenge, when it comes to Boards, is the lack of diversity and expertise in understanding emerging challenges in the environmental and social sphere. Boards are well equipped to handle traditional financial and risk management issues concerning a business. The climate challenge cannot be reduced to these two issues because it has a much broader societal impact. Similarly, CEOs and C-suites are not climate experts, and you need to bring in more of them to advise companies on the transition. Rethinking the Board and management skill sets is going to be quite the challenge.

Q. The ESG space, as you well know, has been consumed with allegations of greenwashing. Do you feel that the sector will recover from what appears to be a series of severe setbacks?

A. We should place this in the appropriate context. Environmental and social issues are a legacy of the global financial crisis – where financial institutions were found to be badly managed, and some were also guilty of selling unethical financial products. The regulatory regime which was established in the aftermath of the GFC has led to a rewiring of financial services and a much more stable and healthy system. In the current context of greenwashing, we are bound to make mistakes but are better positioned to learn from them. There are several positive factors which are converging to address greenwashing. This includes strengthened ESG regulation on issuers, intermediaries, and the rating agencies themselves. We also need to get smarter at due diligence and there is a huge burden on companies which don't have the right data. Regulatory consistency is another important factor, and the work being carried by the Sustainability Accounting Standards Board (SASB) in updating the IFRS regulations as well as the EU taxonomy for sustainable finance will enable this process.

Q. A final question on whether the "S" component of ESG is getting crowded out as business is primarily focused on the climate challenge?

A. There is an element of climate overshadowing the social and governance aspects of ESG. But it is a logical journey – we should effectively deal with emissions first and the other aspects will follow. The focus on nature risks, for example, is an integral part of the "S" pillar because it has huge implications on the habitat and for disadvantaged communities. Diversity and inclusion, as I noted earlier, must be rethought. It is not simply improving diversity in C-suites and Boards but also to ensure that the voices of women and minorities, who are at the frontline of climate distress, are heard and acted upon. The financial sector can contribute by innovating on how we drive financial inclusion. Could we, for example, consider originating carbon credits for local communities and gender empowerment. This will be the true metric of impact investing.

NICK LOVEGROVE

Nick is currently Professor of Practice at Georgetown University's McDonough School of Business, where he teaches courses on management, strategic problem-solving, and principled leadership. I occasionally deliver guest lectures in his classroom. Prior to academia, Nick had a rich and diverse career in consulting (McKinsey & Co, where he was Managing Partner of the D.C. Office, Albright Stonebridge, and Brunswick), public service (he was special advisor to former UK Prime Minister Tony Blair), and in communications. Nick is the author of a fascinating book The Mosaic Principle,[1] *which argues that life – professionally and personally – is*

---

[1] The Mosaic Principle: The Six Dimensions of a Remarkable Life and Career – Nick Lovegrove, Public Affairs, 2017.

lived to the fullest as a mosaic, encompassing a rich and complex set of diverse experiences.

Q. In your under-graduate and graduate classroom, is there significantly greater interest from students on ESG and climate issues and how are universities adapting?

A. I would say yes and frame this as an issue of meeting demand. There is of course a recognition that climate change is the key issue of our time and educators are adapting to ensure that this is integrated into our undergrad and graduate level courses. It is at the same time hard to know if all the demand is met, and this is an ongoing process of integrating environmental and social issues into our curriculum. The business school, for example, has initiated a graduate-level degree in sustainable development.

Q. Is there a clear sense in the student population that ESG issues are core or central to what they will learn?

A. They are eager to learn but of course the student community don't come with high knowledge about the issues. They are not experts, which is not surprising, but want to learn. From what I see in the classroom, this is not an activist generation. One should not generalize because student interests differ based on the program they are pursuing – those pursuing a business degree will have different views compared with students studying foreign policy. Two general observations from me. First, in the American context, the killing of George Floyd in May 2020 ignited an emotional energy about diversity and inclusion issues which is still resonating. This is not necessarily seen as an ESG issue per se but something that our students are passionate about. Second, I have not observed an antipathy toward the establishment, in this case the university. The students are here to learn but they recognize that there are bigger social issues which they are committed and passionate about.

Q. So you don't see this student generation to be in the mold of say their rebellious predecessors of our era?

A. As I noted earlier, there is no student antipathy toward the system and no simmering discontent. One must be careful in drawing sweeping conclusions given their backgrounds and the institution they are studying in. Like every generation, they are driven by career aspirations, but I am confident that when faced with a challenge, they will change.

Q. You were a consultant for much of your career. How radically different is your new job as a professor?

A. There are commonalities and sharp differences as well. For one, there are close interlinkages as they belong to a single ecosystem. However, the personal challenges are different. In teaching, the opportunity is in shaping perceptions, influencing behaviors, and in effect building the leaders of tomorrow. In consulting, there is a difference in methodology and approach of course and there is a constant need to meet market demand with new services through an adaptive business model. I attempt to connect my students to the world of consulting in my classes, providing a glimpse into how business works. Academia is difficult to change because at the core we are bound by the special knowledge of the faculty. It is much more supply and academic lead. The next decade, particularly in America, will shake up universities. There will be a decline in the volume of the incoming student population (due to demographic challenges) and nonelite schools will suffer, as they will have less material resources and agility compared with more established institutions. **We need to build much more robust foundations.**

ACKNOWLEDGMENTS

This book came together due to a combination of good timing and happenstance. Since 2019, my consulting work gave me an opportunity to observe first-hand how companies – public and private, large and small – are dealing with the giant squid that has become ESG. This provided the inspiration and the springboard for the book.

A number of friends, mentors, clients (many of whom prefer to be anonymous), and professional contacts provided me with advice, counsel, pushback, and assistance. They include the following who generously provided the time for the interviews – V, Shankar (Gateway Partners), Deniz Harut (Pollination), and Nick Lovegrove (Georgetown University). I appreciate the support of Gatehouse Partners (Sir Nigel Greenstock, Nick Greenstock); Chatham House (John Kampfner, David Lawrence, Courtney Vance); and the Atlantic Council (Jeremy Mark, Josh Lipsky). I also benefitted from class-room conversations with undergraduate and graduate students at Georgetown University last fall, facilitated by Nick Lovegrove and David Wallis. Thanks as well to the editors at *Forbes* (Rob Olsen, Jeffrey Marcus), *Asia Global Online* (Alejandro Reyes), and *Fortune* (Nicholas Gordon), where I write regularly and previewed some of the themes in the book.

There are a number of other individuals who also provided great insights and provided me with a platform to discuss ESG issues. They include Sunil John and colleagues at BCW (Chad Latz, Stephen Worsley, Dima Maaytah, and Rajeev Nair), Kamar Jaffer, Anil Dua, Andrew Bainbridge, Charles Rigoux, David Fennell, Jessica Keough, Gary Litman, Aziz Mahdi, Rhodri Williams, Rem Korteweg, Champa Patel, Roland Rajah, Nandan Mer, Milan Dalal, Jonathan Charles, and Mark Bergman. My agent, Chris Newson of Newson Wallwork Media did a stellar job in sharpening and successfully pitching the book proposal, and thanks to the terrific team at Emerald Publishing (Nick Wallwork, Thomas Creighton, Kousalya Thangarasu in particular) for bringing the project to fruition. Needless to say, any errors and omissions in the book accrue to me and not to any of the folks listed above and below.

As always, my wife Ferzine and daughter Neha were hugely supportive and remarkably patient, as I squandered the glorious summer of 2022 to finish the book. This book is dedicated to my late mother, who raised me against the odds as a single mom in my formative years and to Singapore, where I got my first break in regional media.

Vasuki Shastry
Washington, DC and Dubai
December 2022

INDEX

AAA (blue-chip company), 143–144
Abu Dhabi's Mubadala, 5–6
Amazon Web Services, 45
American alpha-male capitalism, 29–30
American corporation, 121
American society, 91
Anglo-Saxon model, 56
Apple (company), 99
Artificial intelligence (AI), 128–129
Assets, 69
Australian Securities and Investments Commission (ASIC), 109

Barcelona Olympics, 121
BDO, 109
Biden administration, 32–33
Big Tech firms, 113–114
Bitcoin, 46–47
Black lives matter (BLM), 83
  movement, 83
BlackRock's portfolio companies, 7–8
Boomer generation's signature legacy, 123
Brexit referendum (2016), 8–9
Bridge fuel, 38–39
Buffett's conglomerate, 52–53
Business and profit motive collides with nonfinancial and longer term environmental and social challenges, short-termism in, 49–64

Business community, 4
Business Roundtable (BR), 85–86, 91

Capture process, 72
Carbon
  neutral, 76
  price setting process, 76
Carbon capture, utilization, and storage (CCUS), 71–72
  skeptics, 73–74
  technology, 72–73
Carbon dioxide (CO_2), 19
Central banks, 113
Centre for Climate and Energy Solutions (C2ES), 39–40
Centrifugal force, 136–137
Centripetal forces, 136–137
CEO, 65–79
Chief Financial Officer, The, 66
Chief Risk Officer (CRO), 111–112
Chief Sustainability Officer (CSO), 62, 68
  of DWS, 139–140
Clean Air and Clean Water Acts, 26–27
Climate Action Tracker, 19
Climate activists, 137
Climate change, 32–33
Climate space, 70–71
Codetermination, 133–134
Colonial Oil pipeline shock, 23
Columbia Climate School, The, 46–47
Commissioner, The, 39–40
Confluence Philanthropy, 87–88

Conservative activists, 87
Conventional wisdom, 20
COP26, 37–38
    COP26 climate summit at
        Glasgow, 37
Corporate culture, 60
Corporate power, 87
Corporate Sustainability and
    Reporting Directive
    (CSRD), 89–90
COVID-19, 14, 19–20
Credit rating agencies (CRAs), 143,
    145
Credit rating process, 145–146
CSR, 100

D & O insurance, 104
Depression-era Glass-Steagall Act,
    30
Deutsche Asset Management
    (DWS), 139–141
    funds, 140–141
Divergent approaches, 144
Diversity, 93–96
Diversity and inclusion (D & I), 94
    Europe–0, America–1, 96
    programs, 94
    score as follows, 96–98
    supply chains, 96–98
Drug addicts, 18

Earth Day, 26–27
Economic Policy Institute, The, 14,
    116–117
Economist, The, 42–43, 81–83, 85,
    137
Electrification of mobility, 39–40
Environment Protection Agency
    (EPA), 26–27, 45–46
Environmental, social, governance
    (ESG), 1–16, 82
    complex, 136–137
    consultants complex, 2–3
    ESG-inputs, 138–139
    ESG-linked pay, 117–118
    group of elders have oversight
        over, 103–118

millennials transform
    hidebound culture of
    business and deliver,
    119–134
output funds, 138–139
regulatory framework, 101
Environmental Policy Act, 26–27
Equity analysts, 49–50
Eschews nepotism, 138–139
EU Emissions Trading System (EU
    ETS), 74–75
EU's Sustainable Finance
    Disclosures Regulation
    (SFDR), 140
European approach, 56
European Commission (EC), 39,
    77–78, 92–93
European Commission's Financial
    Services, The, 39
European Council, The, 89–90
European regulators, 89–90
European Union (EU), 56
    law, 89–90
    sustainability taxonomy, 89–90
ExxonMobil (oil company), 72

Financial markets, 137
Financial Times, 8, 50, 138
Fire clouds, 21
Fire-fighting technology, 21
Focusing capital on the long-term
    (FCLT), 52–53
    project, 53
Forum report, The, 44
Fossil fuels sector, 33–34
Friedman doctrine, 27–28
Friedman's theory, 30

Geopolitics, 37–38
Glasgow Financial Alliance for Net
    Zero (GFANZ), 73–74,
    115, 146–147
Global Carbon Project, The, 34–35
Global economy's reliance on all
    things carbon, perverse
    economics behind,
    31–47

Global financial crisis (GFC), 116–117
Global investors, 147–148
Global minimum corporate tax (GMCT), 99–100
Go with the flow (GWTF), 126
Google, 91–92, 128–129
Green metals, 36
Greenpeace, 11–13
Grey London, 8–9
Grime
 every country's great fortune, 17–30
Group of elders have oversight over ESG, 103–118
Guardian, The, 58–59

Hackers, 18–19
Harvard Business Review, 131–133

IMF, 22
Inclusion, 93–96
Indian economy, The, 36
Inflation Reduction Act, 42
Integrity Council for the Voluntary Carbon Market, 76–77
Intergovernmental Panel on Climate Change (IPCC), 20–21, 33–34
 report, 22
International banks, 82–83, 97–98, 146
International community, 23
International Energy Agency (IEA), 25, 44
International Monetary Fund, 4–5
International NGOs, 78, 137
Investing approach, 138–139
Investors, 92, 137
Iranian Revolution, 23
ISS, 140

Key performance indicators (KPIs), 149–150

Laissez faire capitalism, 28
Legacy systems, 113–114
Long-term investor (LTI), 56–57

Malaysia's national oil company, 37
Methane (CH₄), 19
Millennials, 125
 transform hidebound culture of business and deliver ESG, 119–134
MIT Sloan Management Review, 126–127
Modern Slavery Act, 149–150
Monetary Authority of Singapore (MAS), 148–149
Morningstar Sustain analytics, 140
Mortgage-backed securities (MBS), 61
MSCI, 140
Multilateral agencies, 82–83
Multilateral organizations, 22
Multinational companies, 82–83, 97–98
Multinational corporations, 146

National governments, 137
Natural disasters, 19
Natural language processing techniques, 143
Net zero, 76
 emissions, 65–79
Network for Greening the Financial System (NGFS), 112–113
New York Times, The, 24–26, 38–39, 61–62, 83, 95–96
Nongovernmental organization (NGO), 11–12, 66–67
 activism, 121
 campaign, 121
North America Free Trade Agreement (NAFTA), 28–29

Office of the Comptroller of
    Currency (OCC),
    108–109
Organization of Petroleum
    Exporting Countries
    (OPEC), 23

Pandemic, 36–37
Paris Climate accord, 53–54
Payment crisis, 24
Pentagon, 32–33
Perverse economics behind global
    economy's reliance on
    all things carbon,
    31–47
Planting trees, 100
Post, The, 85
Potsdam Institute for Climate
    Impact Research, 35
Pragmatists, The, 71, 77
Principal uncertainty, 111–112
Private-property system, 27
Production process, 44–45, 72
Project Maven, 128–129
Protectors, The, 71, 74–77
Prussian Army, 131–133
Puutu Kunti Kurrama and Pinkura
    people (PKKP), 59–60
PWC (Global consulting firm), 63

Qatar Investment Authority,
    5–6

RAND Corporation, 15
Rebalancing process, 78
Remote workers, 15
Renewable energy, 39–40
Russian Army, 33
Russian invasion, 37–38

S & P Global Corporate
    Sustainability
    Assessment (S & P
    Global Corporate
    CSA), 144
Saudi Arabia's Public Investment
    Fund, 5–6

Science-based Targets Initiative
    (SBTI), 115
Scottish oil company Cairn Energy,
    11–12
Securities and Exchange
    Commission (SEC), 87
Short-termism in business and
    profit motive collides
    with nonfinancial and
    longer term
    environmental and
    social challenges,
    49–64
Silicon Valley, 133
Singapore's central bank, 148–149
Singapore's GIC, 5–6
Socially responsible investing
    investors (SRI
    investors), 96
Sony, 120
Steel manufacturing, 44–45
Streamlined energy and carbon
    reporting (SECR),
    149–150
Supply chains, 96, 98, 100
    Europe–0; America–0, 98
    management, 149–150
    metrics, 98
    social impact, 98–100
Supply crisis, 24
Sustainability, 4–5, 67
    sustainability accounting
        standard board's
        materiality matrix, 2–3
Sustainable finance (SF), 77
Sustainalytics, 117
Swiss bank, 94–95
Systems-based approach, 45–46

Task-force for Climate Financial
    Disclosures (TCFD),
    2–3, 68–69, 105
Taxes, 99–100
Technology, 92–93
Temasek, 5–6
Time and Newsweek, 24
Time magazine, 1
Top Gun movie, 31

Toyota, 120
Treating customers fairly (TCF), 93

U.S. Department of Defense, 31–32
UBS, 94–95
UK's Modern Slavery Act, 90
UN's Department of Economic and
        Social Affairs (DESA),
        142–143
United Nation (UN), 22
    secretary general antonio
        gutteres, 22
    United Nations Climate
        Summit, 120–121
United Nation's Sustainable
        Development Goals
        (SDGs), 1–2, 53–54
United Nations General Assembly
        (UNGA), 130–131
US Armed Forces, 31–33
US Department of Agriculture,
        18–19

Washington Post, The, 85

Watson Institute, 31–32
Wirecard, 50
Woke capitalism, 3, 86–87,
        122–123, 137
    consumer protection, 91, 93, 96
    on diversity & inclusion, score
        as follows, 96–98
    diversity and inclusion, 93–96
    driving companies to focus on
        social justice issues and
        amount to, 81–91
    Europe–0; America–0, 101
    on social impact, 101
    on supply chains, 98–100
World Bank, 36, 82–83
World Economic Forum, The,
        43–44, 150
World Meteorological
        Organization (WMO),
        20
World Trade Organization (WTO),
        35–36

Yom Kippur war, 23

ABOUT THE AUTHOR

Vasuki Shastry is an ESG and strategic communications expert who advises companies in the public and private sector on how to manage and mitigate risks. He was most recently the Global Head of Public Affairs and Sustainability at Standard Chartered Bank in London, where he had oversight over the bank's public policy, sustainability, and environmental/social risk functions. Prior to that, Shastry worked for the International Monetary Fund in Washington, DC. and the Monetary Authority of Singapore (MAS) in leadership roles in communications and public affairs. Besides his passion for ESG, Shastry is also a well-known expert on Asia with a research focus on economic and financial integration, global governance, and climate impact. He is the author of two books on Asia – *Resurgent Indonesia – From Crisis to Confidence* (2018) and *Has Asia Lost It? – Dynamic Past, Turbulent Future* (2021). Shastry is also a Commissioner of the Commonwealth War Graves Commission (CWGC) and divides his time between Washington, DC, and Dubai.